The Barter Theatre Story
Love Made Visible

by Mark Dawidziak

The Appalachian Consortium was a non-profit educational organization composed of institutions and agencies located in Southern Appalachia. From 1973 to 2004, its members published pioneering works in Appalachian studies documenting the history and cultural heritage of the region. The Appalachian Consortium Press was the first publisher devoted solely to the region and many of the works it published remain seminal in the field to this day.

With funding from the Andrew W. Mellon Foundation and the National Endowment for the Humanities through the Humanities Open Book Program, Appalachian State University has published new paperback and open access digital editions of works from the Appalachian Consortium Press.

www.collections.library.appstate.edu/appconsortiumbooks

This work is licensed under a Creative Commons BY-NC-ND license. To view a copy of the license, visit http://creativecommons.org/licenses.

Original copyright © 1982 by the Appalachian Consortium Press.

ISBN (pbk.: alk. Paper): 978-1-4696-3813-3
ISBN (ebook): 978-1-4696-3815-7

Distributed by the University of North Carolina Press
www.uncpress.org

Dedication
For Sara,
For always, forever

FOREWORD

It is with pleasure that I commend this book to you.

It is fitting that THIS book is being published at THIS time. A history of Barter Theatre at a time when Barter Theatre has just completed its 50th—its Golden Anniversary—season of service, a time when Barter Theatre is at a peak period in the artistic quality of its productions and a time when Barter Theatre has expanded into a year round operation, serving not only the Virginia Highlands/East Tennessee region of Appalachia in the spring, summer and fall, but now also serving Northern Virginia with a winter season in Fairfax and other parts of Virginia and surrounding states with an early spring touring season.

It is fitting also that THIS book is primarily about THE MAN, Robert Porterfield, and his association with Barter Theatre, for Barter Theatre was Robert Porterfield in its conception and during its developing years. For forty of its fifty years, Bob - "Mr. P." - put it all together. He produced, directed, designed, acted, promoted Barter Theatre. He gathered together "Friends of Barter," a strong Board of Directors, a Board of Visitors. He attracted financial support and political support. Barter was named "The State Theatre of Virginia." And, before his death, the continuity of Barter Theatre was assured by the creation of Barter Foundation, Inc. to set policy, hold the assets, employ management and assist in financing the theatre. Barter Theatre was and still is Bob Porterfield's creation.

Neither Bob Porterfield nor Barter Theatre achieved preeminence easily. For Barter Theatre, in a town of 5,000 persons, to survive for 50 years—longer than any other professional, regional repertory theatre in the United States; for it to compete for actors, directors, and designers with more than forty other regional professional theatres, all from metropolitan areas of over 300,000 population, has required monumental effort. It has required and has received financial, moral and physical help from hundreds of supporters from throughout the United States.

Barter still faces problems. There is never enough money. Gasoline prices and shortages, tight county, state and federal budgets for the arts, business recession, adverse weather, all present problems which must be overcome but Barter has survived and with careful planning and care will survive to fulfill Barter Theatre's pledge "to combat the evils that would destroy the culture and enlightenment of the world by giving the best of its strength and devotion to the cause of truth, beauty and spiritual nourishment of the human soul."

Fifty years is a good plateau from which to review the past—beginnings, struggles, successes, problems and progress—and to resolve the future—new challenges, new dreams, new effort. This book gives us this 50 year look at Barter Theatre. You will enjoy reading it and Barter Theatre will benefit from your knowing it more intimately.

December, 1982

For the Board of Directors,
The Barter Foundation, Inc.
Fillmore McPherson, Jr., President

Table of Contents

Selected Quotes xi
Introduction xiii
Chapter One: Setting and Scene 3
Chapter Two: Curtain Up 8
Chapter Three: "I'd Rather Entertain Souls" 16
Chapter Four: Ham For Hamlet 21
Chapter Five: Mr. P 29
Chapter Six: The Stars of Barter 47
Chapter Seven: Changes at Barter 71
Chapter Eight: Talking With Owen 89
Chapter Nine: The Ghosts of Barter 93
Chapter Ten: A Day in October 99
Chapter Eleven: The Partington Years 103
Chapter Twelve: The Importance of Being Barter 113
Appendix A: A Code of Ethics for People in the Theatre 117
Appendix B: The Aims and Purposes of the Barter Theatre 118
Appendix C: The Barter Theatre Award 119
Appendix D: Awards and Honors 120
Bibliography and Resources 121

Selected Quotes

Work is love made visible. And if you cannot work with love but only with distaste, it is better that you should leave your work, and sit at the gate of the temple and take alms from those who work with joy.
—Kahil Gibran (quote used for *Robert Porterfield: A Memorial*)

The man with a new idea is a crank, until the idea succeeds.
—Mark Twain

bar*ter (bar'ter) verb. To exchange goods or services without using money. To traffic or trade by exchanging one commodity for another.

Not only will actors benefit from a summer in Virginia but the towns nearby will have Broadway brought to their very doors.
—*Big Stone Gap Post* editorial, 1933.

Admission Price: 30 cents or the equivalent in rations. Bring us honey, fresh eggs, fresh vegetables, hams and other edibles.
—1933 Advertisement for the Barter Theatre's first show.

The Barter Theatre was founded by Robert Porterfield during the depression of 1932.
The original idea of the Barter Theatre was to bring together the hungry actor and the farmer with a surplus of produce.
The Barter Theatre of Virginia, Inc. serves as a non-profit, educational and cultural experiment for the purpose of giving the people of Virginia and its many guest tourists an opportunity to observe some of the works of the world's most distinguished playwrights performed by competent artists.
The Barter Theatre pledges itself to combat the evils that would destroy culture and enlightenment of the world by giving the best of its strength and devotion to the cause of truth, beauty and spiritual nourishment of the human soul.
—Plaque in front of the Barter Theatre.

There's something about this place that keeps drawing you back.
—director Owen Phillips

I think Barter has continued so extremely well because the spirit hasn't changed.
—set designer Lynn Pecktal

If ya' like us, talk about us. If ya' don't, jes keep ya' mouth shut!
—Traditional ending to Robert Porterfield's curtain speech.

Introduction

The arts have always been the realm of long shots, impossible dreams and unrelenting innovators. From the impoverished writer plugging away at a novel or a play to the persevering actor who pounds the New York pavement waiting for the "big" break, the artists, dancers, singers, composers, writers, musicians, comedians and actors strive in professions which dictate the most improbable of odds.

Just to exist day to day, these single-minded professionals must continue to tap an inexhaustable reservoir of belief: belief in the significance of their work, in their own talent, and in the future. It is a world where a nicely worded rejection becomes a comfort or a reason to hope.

In the small Southwest Virginia town of Abingdon there stands a shrine to this uncompromising belief in dreams and the importance of cultural enrichment. It's called the Barter Theatre and its beginnings trace back to the bleakest of all eras for America and the theatre as an institution—the Depression.

The Barter story encompasses many stories. It deals with a training ground that Fritz Weaver calls "the best possible for young actors." It tells how a state government can give and receive much by supporting the arts. It reflects changes and developments in the American theater. It is an integral part of the growth of regional or "decentralized" theater. But, more than anything else, it is the delightful success story of a man and an idea.

Barter's reputation had more than quietly preceded itself to Washington, D.C., where I was working as a journalist in 1978. When informed that I had accepted the post of Arts Editor with the *Bristol Herald-Courier,* several of my more experienced colleagues wagged their heads knowingly and said, "That means you'll be covering the Barter Theatre."

Consequently, I arrived in Bristol—some 15 miles from Abingdon and located on the Virginia-Tennessee border—determined to learn all I could about the Barter Theatre. First step, the local library.

"Let me have your history of the Barter Theatre," I asked.

"Do you know the title or author?"

"No, but whatever it is shouldn't be too difficult to track down," I assured the helpful librarian.

Several minutes later I was informed that they had no such volume on their shelves. Well, I thought, mildly surprised, it's just a small local library. I should have better luck at the Washington County Library in Abingdon. After the above scene was repeated, it all started to sink in. No one had yet published a history of this unique theater.

Still, there was certainly no desire to become Barter's "biographer." That came after a year of watching, listening and learning about Barter and its colorful founder, Robert Porterfield, first with the *Herald-Courier,* then as the critic and entertainment writer for the *Kingsport Times-News.*

First, it just seemed like a great story to tell. Then a few intriguing questions popped up. Just about any Virginia tourism pamphlet will tell you that Barter is the country's longest-running professional resident theater staging plays in America's second oldest theater structure (only the Walnut Street Theatre in Philadelphia is older). Others may tell you that the likes of Edwin Booth, Joseph Jefferson and Fay Templeton appeared on that Abingdon stage. And there are plenty of references to tell you that Robert Porterfield came up with the idea of trading foodstuff for tickets in order to feed hungry actors. Yes, the whos, wheres and whens were fairly well documented. It was the hows and whys that interested me.

How did this quaint little theater again and again turn out such famous names as Hume Cronyn, Frank Lovejoy, Gregory Peck, Patricia Neal, Margaret Phillips, Larry Gates, Margaret Wycherly, Ernest Borgnine, Herbert Nelson, Elizabeth Wilson, Claude Akins, Fritz Weaver, David (Al) Hedison, Grant Williams, Rosemary Murphy, Diane Cilento, Ned Beatty, Robert Pastene, Gerome Ragni, Gary Collins, Mitch Ryan, Larry Linville, David Birney, Richard Sanders and David Selby? How did such a theater survive the Depression in an area with little cultural heritage to speak of to become a heralded example of decentralized theater at its best? Why was the Barter chosen as the first state theater in the country?

After collecting an ungainly mass of notes, clippings, interviews and research, it took quite some time to get a firm grasp on the story I wanted to tell. The meticulous study of scrapbooks and microfilm gave me the skeleton of my work. The interviews and countless pictures provided the flesh and blood. Fortunately, Bob Porterfield left behind many friends and a wealth of write-ups that slowly pieced together answers to those perplexing questions.

Throughout the research, however, I worried about my perspective; a dilemma that I'm glad to report eventually brought me full circle. While the months of groundwork were going by, I was awed by the enormous and seemingly endless mine of Barter history. As the research drew to a close, I realized anew what I had felt at the very start—this is one terrific story. I hope I've done it justice.

Fair warning: the work before you may often read like a fairy tale. That's as it should be, for Barter's record is not only a legacy of good theater; it's the stuff good theater is made of. There are no pretensions of this being a scholarly account of the Barter Theatre or the definitive biography of Bob Porterfield. Instead, my intention is to effect a style that would, I think, have pleased Mr. P.

The spirit of Barter is not a dusty litany of names and dates. Oh, there are passages about the actual practice of Barter, and the social conditions that spawned this distinctive theater, and its impact on the Southwest Virginia-Upper East Tennessee area, and Bob's contributions to the movement for "decentralized" theater, and numerous other worthy aspects that I hope will prove valuable to the students of American theater. Still, Barter is first and foremost what caring, literate theater is all about, and this story will be told as entertainingly as possible.

Introduction   xv

Moving into its 50th year of providing invaluable experience to aspiring performers, Barter is a living, growing monument to its founder, who started his theater with little more than a daring concept, a knack for promotion, a wealth of Southern charm, and 22 starving actors.

To keep these chapters from turning into a dry collection of data, I've tried to sprinkle the narrative with representative Barter fables and legends. In addition to being reflective of Bob and his theater, they give a true feeling for each. On the whole, footnotes tend to be distracting while lending unnecessary weight to a volume. Determined to avoid this plague, an extended list of acknowledgements follows; a chronicle of the many who willingly volunteered hours of time to pause and reminisce, warmly conveying thoughts, memories, ideas, anecdotes and emotions. A more technical compendium of sources and a bibliography can be found in the rear.

First and most affectionately, I acknowledge my debt to Owen Phillips, the man who was a "brother" to Bob and a "godfather" to this work. Owen not only gave this book encouragement, he provided the contagious enthusiasm that must have been effused by Mr. P himself.

My deep gratitude is also extended to Mrs. Mary Dudley Porterfield, a genial, reassuring and gracious contributor. My time at the family estate, Twin Oaks, provided as much a feeling for the man as his theater itself. Her unaffected manner and personal accounts of Bob supplied a perfect complement to the time spent in libraries and newspapers.

Heading the list of friends and advisors to this narrative are Rex Partington, the current artistic director/producer of the Barter Theatre, and Pearl Hayter, business manager and guardian of the many Barter scrapbooks. Frequently during an interview, someone would ask with a wistful smile, "You didn't know Bob, did you?" Admittedly, this was my greatest handicap. However, through these four—Owen, Mary Dudley, Rex and Pearl—I almost get the feeling I did know him.

For their advice and friendship, my thanks to Barter publicity director Lou Flanigan, Lynn Pecktal and Frank Lowe.

Although no book has ever been published on the Barter Theatre, my way was well blazoned by two exhaustive theses. The first Anne St. Clair Williams' painstakingly detailed 1970 doctoral thesis, *Robert Porterfield's Barter Theatre of Abingdon, Virginia*, an indispensable survey and analysis. Affectionately known as "the Red Book," St. Clair's effort is "the" definitive chronicle of Barter events up to Bob's death. It's a shame her thesis hasn't come to popular light. Luckily for me, we did manage to consume several cups of coffee while brainstorming about Barter. For once, I shut up and listened. As Barter's historian, many of her comments are included. The second thesis is *A Survey of the Attitudes of the Abingdon Community Toward Barter Theatre* by Teresa Diane Keller, who also consented to be interviewed about her research and the time she spent working in the Barter's publicity office.

It would be impossible to list all those who furnished bits of information and vital pieces of Barter history, but special thanks are gratefully extended to Hume Cronyn, Fritz Weaver, Ned Beatty, Claude Akins, Mitch Ryan, David Selby, Bob Gallico, Cleo Holladay, Mrs. Owen (Ruth) Phillips, Jeff Meredith, Betsy Graham, Woody Vance, Becky Rose, Lily Lodge, Russell Gold, Leta Bonynge, F. Leonard Darby, David M. Lohoefer, Ann Buckles, Peter Culman and Harry Ellerbe.

Also grateful thanks to the *Kingsport Times-News*, the *Bristol Herald-Courier*, and the *Washington County News* for the use of their files and resources.

I hope they all liked talking to me about Bob and Barter and, together, I hope we can get some more people talking about it.

Mark Dawidziak

The Barter Theatre Story
Love Made Visible

Perhaps the most famous picture of Robert Porterfield, this warm study shows Barter's founder sitting among the seats from the Empire Theatre, each bearing an ornate needlepoint 'E'.
(Photo courtesy of the Barter Theatre)

Chapter One: Setting and Scene

Any good piece of theater should adequately set the time and place.
The Great Depression—1933.
It was no time to be an aspiring actor in New York. The Depression had reached its lowest ebb.

Since the early part of the century, the American theater had become increasingly centralized in an area of Manhattan known as Broadway. Indeed, "The Great White Way" has established itself alongside Berlin, Paris and London as an international cultural capital. To many, the American theater and Broadway were synonymous. So, when the country's economic collapse ravaged the city, the toll was dearly felt on the American theater as an institution.

With fewer dollars to be spent, ticket sales plummeted along with the number of productions. Broadway producers and managers, natural speculators in the stock market, had suffered enormous losses and few chances were being taken on either new playwrights or performers. Some producers, such as Sam Harris and the Schuberts, managed to weather the storm. Others, notably Arthur Hammerstein and A.H. Woods, declared bankruptcy. Flo Zigfield, one of Broadway's greatest names, was wiped out.

"Nowadays," went comedian Eddie Cantor's ominous observation after the Stock Market crashed, "when a man walks into a hotel and requests a room on the 19th floor, the clerk asks him, 'For sleeping or jumping?' "

Cantor had little reason to laugh. He was only one in a legion of Broadway actors, playwrights, directors and producers who had literally lost entire fortunes overnight. The walking wounded included such prominent theatrical figures as Harris, George S. Kaufman, Alexander Woollcott, Irving Berlin, Groucho Marx and Max Gordon. Groucho would later recall with more than just a touch of bitterness how he starred in the "Follies of 1929."

Movies—motion pictures, films, the flickers, talkies—were a cheaper and more productive form of entertainment, and Broadway, Vaudeville and the legitimate theater felt the impact of this rising popularity.

Stars and "big names," however, could easily launch into new projects and recoup their losses. As galling or demoralizing as the loss of personal fortunes were to Broadway's elite, they had one financial advantage—their reputations. It was the rank and file actor who was particularly hard hit. The words "Buddy, Can You Spare a Dime?" seemed to sum up the stark city environment of breadlines and corner applecarts run by former Wall Street wizards.

Author and columnist Heywood Broun, deeply disturbed by the growing deprivation in the Broadway sector, helped produce a revue to benefit out-of-work troupers. Despite the affable writer's sincere intentions, *Shoot the Works* had a short run and did little to help the unemployed actor.

On a more practical level, the Stage Relief Fund desperately tried to cope with alarming unemployment. By 1933, the Actor's Dinner Club had been set up in the basement of New York's Union Methodist Church to offer balanced meals to less fortunate thespians. Years later, Bob Porterfield would recall taking advantage of these cheap meals and the opportunity to trade shop-talk with his fellow actors.

Still, in spite of all the grim developments, 1933 brought the first real reason for hope since the crash of '29—better known in theatrical circles by the *Variety* headline, "Wall St. Lays An Egg." Although the country would never really pull out of the Depression until World War II stimulated the economy, the inauguration of Franklin Delano Roosevelt as 32nd president made many feel that "happy days" were indeed here again.

Roosevelt declared a bank holiday one day after his March 4 inauguration ceremony and set the NRA into action. Compared to Herbert Hoover's quiet brand of leadership, this whirlwind of activity gave the nation a sense of recovery.

It was 1933 and a still unknown novelist named John Steinbeck had published a poorly received work titled, *To A God Unknown*. Groucho, Harpo, Chico and Zeppo released their last film as "The Four Marx Brothers," a wild satire on war concocted by Bert Kalmar and Harry Ruby, *Duck Soup*. Perhaps their greatest film, it too was trounced by the critics.

Tobacco Road, a shocking play of human degradation, became the talk of Broadway, while two of New York's wickedest wits, Messrs. Kaufman and Woollcott, teamed up for the disappointing *The Dark Tower*.

Richard Rodgers and Lorenz Hart had temporarily left Broadway for some lucrative movie offers. Hollywood had stepped up its efforts to provide escapist entertainment to a Depression-weary nation and in 1933...skinny Stan Laurel and tubby Oliver Hardy sneaked off to the *Sons of the Desert* convention, telling their wives they were going to Hawaii for their health. Meanwhile, *King Kong* carried the lovely Fay Wray to the top of the Empire State Building; Claude Rains pulled his disappearing act in *The Invisible Man*; Walt Disney was delighting audiences with an average of two Mickey Mouse cartoons each month; Wallace Beery and Marie Dressler recaptured their wonderful *Min and Bill* chemistry with *Tugboat Annie*; premiere Broadway dancer Fred Astaire made his film debut opposite Joan Crawford, Clark Gable, and the Three Stooges in *Dancing Lady*; Frank Capra, a former gagman for Mack Sennett, garnered some increased respect as a director with his *Lady for a Day*; James Cagney showed he was more than just a tough-guy gangster type by tap dancing his way through *Footlight Parade*; and sultry Mae West sang "A Guy What Takes His Time" in *She Done Him Wrong*, a spoof which co-starred an up-and-coming Cary Grant.

For those who preferred to stay at home for their entertainment, Kate Smith,

Rudy Vallee and Paul Whiteman made up the vanguard of radio's musical stars, with Amos n' Andy, Ed Wynn and Fred Allen offering humorous interludes, and Clem McCarthy and Mel Allen handling the sportscasting duties.

Golfing great Bobby Jones was in Augusta, Georgia, laying the foundation for a tournament that would eventually draw international attention. It would be called simply, The Masters. A pathetic Italian giant named Primo Carnera, owned and manipulated by the mob, sat on the heavyweight boxing throne. The most inept of all champions, he would be knocked to the canvas eleven times the following year against an opponent "the boys" could not buy off: Max Baer. Baseball was still the national pastime and the New York Yankees its premiere team, although the year before seemed to be the last truly great season for the Bronx Bombers of Ruth, Gehrig and Dickey.

A survey revealed that reading had become America's favorite form of recreation. Radio placed second, while films ran third. Although entertainment and sports thrived in a nation escaping the harsh realities of the Depression, there were enough fads and headlines to capture the country's imagination.

Jigsaw puzzles became a fad in 1933, along with long fingernails popularized by Marlene Dietrich. Columnists ruled the newspaper world, with Walter Winchell, Westbrook Pegler, Broun and Franklin Pierce Adams leading the pack. And a new weekly news magazine, appropriately titled *Newsweek*, hit the stands with its breezy, summary format.

Prohibition was repealed in 1933 and the "great experiment" was relegated to a select list of notorious historical failures.

The man behind the kidnapping and murder of the Lindbergh baby a year earlier was still at large, as was John Dillinger. In New York, mobster Dutch Schultz was recklessly continuing his ill-fated rise to power. Somewhat more calculating, Charles "Lucky" Luciano was figuring out a way to put the "organized" into "organized crime."

A man with a Charlie Chaplin moustache had consolidated his power in Germany to the point of total authority. With Germany under his thumb, Adolf Hitler would soon look to other countries to conquer. On another continent, Japan reached out to invade the area of China known as Manchuria, setting into motion the series of events that would culminate in World War II.

And into this atmosphere of a world exploding with change in 1933, the Barter Theatre opened its doors in Abingdon, a town rapid change had passed by....

Abingdon: one of the oldest communities in the Southwest region of Virginia. It first appeared on a map by surveyor Thomas Lewis as "Burkes Garden." The site was renamed by no less than Daniel Boone, who camped there during his first trip westward about 1760. According to legend, Boone and his companion, Nathaniel Gist—who were forging the famed "Wilderness Trail" to Kentucky—made camp at a spring near where the present county jail is located, only to have their dogs attacked by a wolf pack from a nearby cave. The wolves' den at the crest of a hill is now the location of the Cave House, a well-known local landmark. Abingdon's first official name thus became Wolf Hill.

Since Wolf Hill naturally became a "crossroads to the West," an actual village was quickly established, complete with a church. But the very first building erected was a powder magazine, later a courthouse leveled by Northern troops in 1864. When a fort was constructed in 1776 on Captain Joseph Black's farm, Wolf Hill became Black's Fort—a distribution point for mail and supplies. And, that same year, the Virginia General Assembly named the settlement the seat of the newly established Washington County, named after the general from Virginia early in the struggle for independence and long before he was acknowledged as "The Father of his Country." The General Assembly also changed the name of Black's Fort to Abingdon in October, 1778.

Some feel the name came from the Duke of Abingdon by way of friends in the area. Still others contend it was simply taken by pioneers from the town of Abingdon in England. Most, however, say "it was named after a parish in which Martha Washington worshipped as a girl."

Southwest Virginia's first post office was established in Abingdon in 1793, the only post office in Washington County as late as 1833.

"By the late 1830s," reads one widely distributed local history, "Abingdon had grown to be an established merchant town with hotels and taverns for the wagonmasters, mercantile houses, tanyards, grocers, wheelwrights, blacksmiths, shoemakers, house carpenters, stone masons, bricklayers, jewelers, and one millinery shop. It had everything the settlers further west would want from the civilized east, plus all the things demanded by the merchants and their families."

"Creating the atmosphere of the town," the narrative continues, "are the buildings from Abingdon's past. The McDonald Tavern on East Main Street is the oldest building in Abingdon, built in 1779. On Court Street is the first brick dwelling, built for William King in 1803. Other beautiful homes line Main Street, one of the most famous being the General Francis Preston home, built between 1830 and 1832, which is now the center building of the Martha Washington Inn."

Actually, the stately Preston home was turned into the Martha Washington College for Girls in 1853. It was temporarily used as a hospital during the Civil War. Another school, the Stonewall Jackson Institute for Women, eventually set up offices and classrooms on a hillside several blocks from Main Street about the turn of the century.

An industry boom hit the surrounding towns in the 1880s, but Abingdon remained a small, elegant community tucked in the beautiful, rolling hills of Southwest Virginia. Located in a fertile valley between the Blue Ridge and Appalachian Mountains; lying between two main forks of the Holston River; and in the shadow of Mount Rogers, Virginia's highest peak, Abingdon existed through farming—mainly dairy, tobacco, cattle and poultry—very light industry and its two colleges.

In 1930, Abingdon was near four "good-sized towns": Bristol, Tennessee-

Virginia, a railroad center with a state line running down its main street and a focal point for a five-state area; Johnson City, Tenn., the largest with a population of 25,000; Kingsport, Tenn., the home of the growing Tennessee Eastman photochemical plant; and Elizabethton, Tenn.

The area boasted little in the way of cultural heritage, with the exception of an already national reputation for country-western music. Indeed, when the Victor Talking Machine Company sent representative Ralph Peer to "the mountains" in 1927 to audition "hillbilly" talent, the moon-faced agent set up shop in Bristol. The surrounding hills and hollows of Appalachia echoed with the sound of grassroots music made by generations of families on crude, handcrafted instruments. The nasal lyrics sprung from an isolated existence spent working in the coal mines of Southwest Virginia, laboring on the railroad lines, scratching a living from a sometime fertile, sometime rocky soil, and praising the Lord from a pine pew. Records, once all the rage, were being threatened by the popularity of radio, and the major recording labels were scrambling to find new and fresh artists to boost dwindling sales. Into Peer's makeshift studio strode Jimmie Rodgers and the Carter Family—A.P., Maybelle and Sara. Those 1927 recordings made in Bristol started a national craze for country music. The event is recognized as the birth of the country-western music industry.

Still, inhabitants of the region saw nothing special in either Rodgers or the Carter Family. And it was hard to fathom all the fuss being made by the rest of the country. Music was a way of life, but it was certainly no way to make a living. Or, as one old saying went, "a man who played the banjo wasn't worth the bullet to shoot him." Although Southwest Virginia and Upper East Tennessee were the richest areas for musicians and country songs, it was all taken for granted and the industry soon set up headquarters some 300 miles away in Nashville.

Mainly descended from Scottish, Irish and English stock, the residents of this area were extremely religious—Presbyterian, Baptists, Methodists. To them, music was for singing in church, humming in the fields, or playing during Saturday night get-togethers in the kitchen. Ironically, it was their hymns and rich folk music heritage that served as a cornerstone for so much of the growing country-western music field.

As for the stage, it was considered a wicked place—the playground of the devil, "the legs of Satan." An actor was a shiftless no-account who couldn't make an honest living. Into Abingdon, into this time, into this environment, arrived Bob Porterfield and his company of New York actors in 1933.

Chapter Two: Curtain Up

"We're going to church!"

Robert Porterfield's announcement stunned the 22 New York actors who had followed the charistmatic "Mr. P" to a remote town in Southwest Virginia. The idea of stage performers trekking all the way to some unheard of place called Abingdon was crazy enough, but now—attending Sunday morning services?

It was the spring of 1933. Abingdon could not have been further removed from the bleak city these performers had just left. They were a mixed bag of theater veterans, newcomers, leading men, ingenues, and character actors. These creators and inhabitants of make-believe worlds all shared one soberingly realistic experience: They had all been touched by the devastation of the New York theater by the Depression. No amount of talent, experience or enthusiasm, they found out, were safeguards against hunger and breadlines.

Food was hardly a problem in Abingdon, population 2,000. In fact, the fertile hills of Washington County had yielded local farmers an excess of crops that they could not sell because of a depressed market. Thus, Porterfield reasoned, the residents of this rural area would gladly "barter" foodstuffs for theater. But first, he had to sell the troupe to the town. He had to convince the community that these decadent theater people were in reality just plain folk.

Abingdon was far removed from the big city scene and sentiment by more than several hundred miles. The town's architecture retained much of the Old South charm, and its citizens held to the Old South outlook. Natives still talked with resentment of how the "Yankees" had sacked Abingdon during the "War Between the States." The term "Civil War" was enough to draw indignant stares from the locals and label one an outsider.

The red brick Oprey House dated back to the early 1830s, originally built as the new Sinking Spring Presbyterian Church, later falling into the hands of the Sons of Temperance and becoming widely known as the Temperance Hall. The first known theatrical production in the structure was *The Virginian* on January 14, 1876, and the likes of Edwin Booth, Fay Templeton and Joseph Jefferson were said to have graced its stage. With the dawn of a new century, the two surviving trustees of the Sons of Temperance turned over the Temperance Hall to the town of Abingdon. When Porterfield arranged to use the hall for the debut of his new company, the town hall was upstairs while the jail occupied the basement. Across the street stood a sprawling mansion—the defunct Martha Washington College—where Porterfield's actors had taken up residence. A stately reminder, it epitomized the grandeur and grace of a revered but bygone era and housed the out-of-town delegation.

Abingdon, in short, was the last place 22 "Yankee" actors would have chosen to take their bows. Yet Porterfield's vision, the Barter Theatre, was the alternative to no work and no food. The idea of playing Shakespeare to farmers was somewhat more attractive than starving, and if Porterfield said they were going to church, they would go.

There was a method to his madness. Porterfield, an ambitious 27, was no Yankee and he understood what the presence of actors meant in Abingdon. The tall, ruggedly handsome founder of Barter, who grew up in nearby Saltville, wanted to show his skeptical neighbors that "the theater and the church were not necessarily at the opposite ends of the street."

So on the Sunday before his Barter Theatre's opening night, Porterfield marched his actors from their residence at the old Martha Washington College, down Main Street to the Presbyterian Church.

Staid churchgoers raised dubious eyebrows as the performers quietly settled into the back pews. They remained stoically unconvinced until it came time for the hymns. Booming over the rest of the congregation was the beautiful baritone of H.H. McCollum. Not only did he bring moving expression to the words of "Rock of Ages," but he sang without a hymn book, as only a real Christian could.

In that instant, Abingdon took Bob Porterfield's Barter troupe to its heart. After services, each actor was invited to someone's home for lunch. The Barter Theatre was a hit before the first play was presented. And no amount of public relations could ever match what that one trip to church accomplished.

Later, when Porterfield complimented McCollum on his powerful rendition, the actor confided to his boss, "The reason I knew the verses is because I had to know them in a play last year. I haven't been to church in 25 years."

The first of many colorful tales this unique company would produce, this particular story illustrates Porterfield's sensitivity to the town and his legendary gift for promotion—two of the principal reasons why the Barter survived.

As another Barter legend goes, Porterfield was on tour with Walter Hampden's famous company of *Cyrano de Bergerac* when the inspiration to trade "ham for Hamlet" occured to him. After a West Coast engagement, the actors' train was headed across the wheat fields of Kansas. The young actor gazed at the passing farmlands and started thinking out loud about the abundance of crops in his native Southwest Virginia. It was ironic, he told Hampden, that so many actors went without food while many farmers had produce rotting in their fields because they couldn't sell it. And for the most part, he continued, these farmers were starved for culture. Would it be possible to operate a theater by having those farmers exchange produce and foodstuffs for tickets to shows?

Hampden didn't think much of the idea. After all, he pointed out, most actors thought of produce as something thrown at them by hostile audiences.

Still, the idea for the Barter Theatre was sparked. Bartering was not uncommon in the hills of Virginia. One of the earliest known systems of exchange in civilization, barter has generally enjoyed increased popularity during times of economic instability. Not suprisingly, many turned to the practice during the Depression out of necessity.

And there was certainly an abundance of potatoes, apple butter and aged hams at the Porterfield family farm, Twin Oaks, near Glade Spring. Why not work a trade?

His mother had kept Bob up to date on the latest news from home and his idea for a "barter" theater was helped along when he heard that both the Martha Washington College and Stonewall Jackson Institute in Abingdon had closed. All those rooms and facilities just going to waste. And there was the Oprey House in Abingdon. All signs were pointing to Abingdon as the site for "Bob's idea."

Between working such odd jobs as elevator boy at the New York Athletic Club and modeling, Bob wrote the trustees of both colleges and the Abingdon Town Council, explaining his idea and outlining what he needed to pull it all off. The response was better than he dared hope. Bob got the Martha Washington College building free of charge, with just utility bills and upkeep to worry about. The Stonewall Jackson facilities were offered for a nominal rent. Abington officials, receptive to new ideas that would stimulate a dismal economic scene, kicked in the opera house free, providing no shows would be given on Sunday.

Other "agreements" were made in New York, where Bob had no shortage of "theater" friends. Actor's Equity agreed to allow performers to appear in the Virginia Highlands, endorsing Bob's plan fully since it could keep some actors from starving. The Actor's Relief Fund also gave Bob its enthusiastic backing and he promised the beneficent organization a share of any profits. And the Dramatics Guild, at playwright Austin Strong's suggestion, allowed the new Barter company to produce any of its plays with only a Virginia ham as payment for royalties. This unique theater tradition was followed by the like of Noel Coward, Thornton Wilder, Robert E. Sherwood, and Maxwell Anderson.

Despite all the encouragement and cooperation, Barter was still a long shot. Porterfield repeated his brainstorm to some New York friends who received the plan with good-natured disbelief.

"Well," he retorted, "Down where I come from in Southwest Virginia, they've always been great people for swapping or bartering."

Shaking her head, the great Broadway actress Jane Cowl handed him a statuette. "Bob," she explained, "this is Saint Rita, patron saint of the impossible. Carry it with you and if by chance you succeed, pass it along to someone else who is attempting the impossible."

Undaunted, Porterfield arrived in Abingdon on May 22, 1933 with St. Rita, some scenery he picked up from a bankrupt road company of *Rose Marie* and his 22 performers in hot pursuit.

In that first company appeared such names as Eleanor Powers, Robert Thomsen, Agnes Ives, Charles Powers, Mildred Quigley, Nell Harrison, Bob Fogle, Emily Woodruff, Munsey Slack, Marjorie Lutz, Hugh Millard, Ruth Guitterman and Storrs Haynes.

Bob certainly hit with four indispensible members of the company. Helen Rhone Fritch, a faculty member of the Martha Washington College whom close friends called "Fritchie," became something of a business manager for Porterfield. She supervised the actors' lodgings, meals, and the box office. In a short time she'd also become Mrs. Robert Porterfield. Years later, people would remember "Fritchie" as the "one who watched the pennies." If you absolutely needed something, you got it, but you had to justify the use of funds or material.

"You could spend a dime wisely and she was enthusiastic," director Owen Phillips explained, "but she was furious if you spent a nickel foolishly."

The second person Bob depended on during that first year for day to day survival was non-stop publicity machine, Ricky Austin. Having worked in newspapers and publicity in both New York and California, Austin was also an aspiring performer in plays and films. Thoughout 1933, Barter's publicity director saturated the area newspapers with an impressive string of features, profiles, announcements and news releases. In addition to concentrating on the media in the 15-to-100-mile touring radius, Austin capitalized on Barter's colorful and unique operation by garnering international attention through features in the *New York Times*, *Variety*, the *Baltimore Sun*, *Richmond Times-Dispatch*, *Washington Post* and even the *London Times*. A mere glance at the public relations generated by Austin demonstrates quite convincingly how fortunate Porterfield was to have a person on staff who recognized Barter's natural promotional worth.

Also of great help were actor-director Prentice Abbot and stage manager Robert Fogle, both of whom brought years of stock, touring and New York experience with them.

But it was Bob's personality that kept everything going, even at the most discouraging moments. There could be no stars in the pampered sense and everyone was expected to help build sets, gather props, construct costumes, and do whatever they could just to make sure there would be a tomorrow for the Barter Theatre. And somehow, even with unknown audiences and a torturous touring schedule facing them, Bob convinced them it would all work.

Before the curtain went up on Barter's first production, Porterfield was moving at an incredibly industrious pace, setting the example for his company. After drawing up a tentative touring schedule, he set out to make sure his Barter Theatre would have an audience.

"He personally built interest in Barter by visiting the civic leaders, newspaper editors, groups and organizations," stated Barter scholar Anne St. Clair Williams. "He checked out the various halls, theaters and auditoriums in the area; although in some cases, they were appearing in gymnasiums or libraries. Some towns booked the whole season of plays, while others just took one or two. Bob was great in front of an audience, but he was unbeatable one-on-one. That's what built this company—that and the cohesive nature of the company. They were all playing for the success of the theater. That feeling of ensemble was

Robert Porterfield and a direct descendant and her descendants of the original pig turned in as "barter" on the Barter Theatre's opening night, June 10, 1933.
(Photo courtesy of the Barter Theatre)

what kept people coming back."

"There's no star complex around here," Bob would assure years after Barter opened.

Posters were placed around town proclaiming: "With vegetables you cannot sell, you can buy a good laugh." On June 10, 1933, the Barter Theatre opened its doors with John Golden's *After Tomorrow*. For the rest of the summer, the company traveled to nearby Kingsport and Johnson City, Tenn., as well as Gate City, Chilhowie, Damascus, Glade Spring, Emory, Wytheville and Bristol. Admission was 30 cents or the equivalent in eggs, honey, fruits, vegetables, hams and other foodstuffs.

Legend has it that the first item brought to the box office was the sow pig that became Barter's mascot and whose descendants provided royalties for several seasons of Barter productions.

"That one pig has done more for the drama than any individual or institution," Bob declared some time later. "If the theater gets so much support from the makers of ham, we should support the hams better."

"We play six nights a week," Porterfield related during those early days, "moving around from one barn or schoolhouse to another, within a radius of 70 miles. But we always come back to Abingdon for the night, riding in an old bus called Bessie, with the evening's box office returns in our laps."

With the company scrambling to mount each new show, Austin was providing show-by-show material, including profiles on featured performers and feature articles on productions. A total of seven plays were offered that first season: *After Tomorrow*, *Salt Water* by Dan Jarrett, *Caught Wet* by Rachel Roberts, *Three Wise Fools* by Austin Strong, *East Lynne* by Mrs. Henry Wood, and the premier productions of *The Bob-Tailed Nag* by Frances Mallor and *Monkey Hat* by Tom Powers, which Porterfield himself appeared in.

If the titles were less than memorable, Bob's audiences certainly didn't seem to mind. "Bring us honey, fresh eggs, fresh vegetables, hams and other edibles," Barter asked, and a culture-starved populace responded.

At home, the reaction was overwhelmingly favorable. "That their engagement has been successful," wrote the *Bristol News Bulletin* at the end of the first season, "is proven by the plans that are being made to return again next year with bigger and better entertainments for their Virginia audience....Just as Martha Graham and her group of dancers are striving to bring to dance a new meaning, so the Barter Theatre group hopes in time to present subtler, more educational dramas for the public they have built up here in the South, away from the sometimes decadent effect of the more hardened New York stage."

The view of "decadent" New York may have been somewhat harsh, but the acknowledgement of Barter's success is well noted. On a more restrained note, the *Big Stone Gap Post* praised Bob, saying his idea "is well conceived. Not only will actors benefit from a summer in Virginia but the towns nearby will have Broadway brought to their very doors."

Under an editorial titled "Something New For Us," the *Gate City Herald* commented, "The taking over of the Martha Washington Inn as summer headquarters for actors and actresses is something new for this section (of the country).... In the giving of these plays to rural audiences, we see a great chance for the education of the people in what constitutes skilled acting."

And Barter was also news nationwide. At a time when most newspaper and radio reports gave the country little reason for cheer, Bob's spunk and Barter's novelty was not lost on feature writers and news organizations. The *Richmond Times-Dispatch* wrote that Barter had offered a "new deal" for the words "ham" and "actor." In its typically show businessy way, *Variety* ran a front-page feature carrying the headline: "Drammer to Billies."

Barter was also featured in a Paramount newsreel, and the *Baltimore Sun* published a page-one story from the letters of Robert Thomsen, a young Baltimore resident who acted with the company during the first season. "I never in all my life had a better time," he wrote. "People started appearing with 'barter' about eleven o'clock and by the middle of the afternoon, the box office was filled with the most amazing lot of stuff. The first ticket was bought with a very small baby pig that can defeat any actor's voice. We got enough onions to keep a century, lettuce, corn, a chocolate cake and the biggest black rooster I ever saw. It was the strangest sight—these farmers coming up to the box office and handing over livestock and vegetables for a ticket."

And so the stories and legends started to circulate that would lend Barter with so singular a reputation among theaters. Years later, Bob would say that no matter where he traveled in the world, he always met somebody who knew about his Barter Theatre.

Since money was hardly in excess during that first season, Bob put the accent on acting rather than props, costumes, scenery and lighting. He had arrived in Abingdon with the *Rose Marie* scenery, which was reworked for several shows.

"They got by with the minimum," Anne St. Clair Williams pointed out. "Actors wore their own clothes on stage whenever possible, and people in Abingdon donated clothes and furniture regularly. Other pieces were borrowed for a particular play and even the furnishings of the Martha Washington Inn were used."

"The first year we had only one set," Porterfield would later recall," and after each Saturday night performance that set had to be reconstructed for the Monday night opening of a new play."

Yet, no matter how hard the day-to-day toil was, nobody was going hungry. Porterfield had found the answer in barter.

"There has always been a great deal of bartering in Virginia," he told the *New York Herald-Tribune*. "So when the Depression came along, and I began to think of starting a summer theatre, it was only natural that I should try to incorporate barter an an essential feature of the scheme.

"Determining a fair price for a ticket, when one person brings in a ham, the next a sack of potatoes and a third a dozen eggs, isn't always easy. Mostly we use the market price of the community as a basis of reckoning. When the offering is insufficient, the playgoer is told to bring some more next time—that is when he

Curtain Up 15

A typical Barter Theatre box office take during the first season in 1933.
(Photo courtesy of the Barter Theatre)

can be trusted. Luckily, I grew up in Abingdon and I know who's who."

On still another occasion, Bob would say of 1933: "I distinctly remember the first year in Abingdon. All the banks in the country were closed, yet the people gathered their garden truck and came to the plays. The mayor and the president of the bank both thanked me for bringing the Barter Theatre to Abingdon. They said, 'until tonight, everyone in town has been depressed about the banks closing, but now their interest has perked-up.' "

That first year resulted in a grand profit of $4.30—promptly turned over to the Actor's Relief Fund—and a company of well-fed performers. Indeed, Bob estimated that the troupe had gained a total of 300 pounds in weight; an average of ten pounds an actor. Nobody had really grown rich, except area residents in a cultural sense and the actors in unforgettable experience. The Barter Theatre was a success and the country had begun to take notice.

Bob celebrated by marrying Helen Fritch in February of 1934 in New York.

Chapter Three: "I'd Rather Entertain Souls"

The earliest mention of a Porterfield ancestor is in a charter dated 1160 to Alanus de Porter. Apparently, he was one of 20 Scots nobles used as hostages by King Henry II of England in seeing that the 1174 Treaty of Falaise be observed. Later, John Porterfield, the son of Robert Porter, had the lands of Porterfield confirmed to him on February 3, 1460.

In his 1947 genealogy, *The Porterfields*, Frank B. Porterfield traces the family's origins and eventual emigration from Scotland to the United States and Virginia. His impressive work details all the Porterfields of prominence over the centuries. Hardly the most conspicuous or exhaustive entry is the one for Robert Huffard Porterfield on page 159. The passage notes that he is "the originator of the Barter Theater (sic)...the only theater in the world to which people trade victuals for entertainment." Then, with scholarly understatement, Frank added that "his theater has received much favorable newspaper comment."

The odds against Bob Porterfield becoming an actor were about as great as the chances his theater would survive 1933. He was born on December 21, 1905 in Wythe County, Virginia, near the industrial camp of Austinville—the location usually given for his birth. Bob was the third of six boys, one of whom died in infancy. His father, William B. Porterfield Sr., eventually took a job managing a 20,000-acre farm in Saltville, and moved his wife and five children "to the first home Bob Porterfield really remembered."

It was in Saltville that Bob "grew up and loved and fought and went to school and acquired most of the ideals and ambition and common sense that have stood me in good stead ever since." Although he would later admit to being an "aloof" youngster at times, Bob's childhood memories were typical of rural Southwest Virginia in the early 20th century: milking cows, hogkilling, grooming horses, harvest times, pitching hay, smoking hams, curing bacon, Saturday afternoon haircuts by Dad with oatmeal bowls over the head, the one-room schoolhouse, coon hunting, the first phonograph in the parlor, and, perhaps most important, amateur theatrics in the barn.

Bales of hay were his first proscenium arch. A horse blanket was his first curtain. His father's barn was his first theater. And his cousins were his first audience. That was when he was seven.

"When I was ten-years-old," he once recalled, "I dreamed one night I was going to be an actor. The dream was very real and showed me many of the things I must do to achieve my goal. When I woke up I knew I would one day be an actor. The dream has come true in great part and I hope the rest of it which hasn't yet been fulfilled will be in time."

"I'd Rather Entertain Souls"

By the age of 12, young Bob had no doubts about his profession and he stunned his family by announcing his intention to become an actor while breakfast was being served.

His father, who wanted him to be a preacher, was emphatic.

"You are not going into that wicked world of theater," he decreed.

His devoted mother, Miss Daisy, calmly said, "We'll see what happens."

Both parents undoubtedly believed this was merely a romantic childhood ambition that he would grow out of sooner or later. Bob's dream did not die, however, and he was fortunate enough to have teachers that instilled a love of reading that remained with him for the rest of his life. As a young student, he couldn't seem to get enough books—history, almanacs, poetry, encyclopedias, anything. Invariably, everyone from politicians to farmers were impressed with Bob's ability to talk knowledgeably on any topic. And any aversion to the classics was lost through a teacher's Shakespeare quotation bees. He also became increasingly interested in oratory and on May 31, 1924, the gangly Saltville High School senior won a Ninth District oratorical contest in Bristol. His topic, "Jefferson and the Constitution," placed second at the state finals in Richmond, although Bob thought "I should have won."

Before graduation, he helped produce *Julius Caesar* and played Brutus: an event that reaffirmed his love for the stage. Bob then spent two years at Hampden-Sydney College in supposed preparation for the ministry. To his father's dismay, it didn't work out that way.

Apparently, the clincher occured when 19-year-old Bob traveled to Richmond for a debate tournament. He saw his first professional company at the old Lyric Theatre—the road show of *Rose Marie*—and all thoughts of the ministry vanished in the glare of reflected stage lights. He made up his mind. He would leave Hampden-Sydney and pursue his dream.

One of his professors tried to talk him out of it by describing at length the beauty of saving souls.

"Sir," Bob told him, "I'd rather entertain souls than save them."

The aspiring actor applied at New York's Academy of Dramatic Arts and soda jerked in a Petersburg drugstore while waiting for an answer. A letter of acceptance arrived at the same time as a note from his father demanding he return home or go back to school. He would go to New York, but first there would be a trip home under doctor's orders.

His father, well aware of Bob's fierce resolve, asked the diagnostician to disuade him. After several long talks with his patient, the diagnostician told the elder Porterfield, "I never examined a healthier patient that had ambition. Why don't you let the boy do what he wants to?"

Grudgingly, his father gave in.

Bob's accent became a cause celebre among instructors at the Academy of Dramatic Arts. To help rid him of his Southern inflections, they strictly forbade any contact with Southerners. It worked to their satisfaction and Bob made his Broadway debut in a walk-on part the night after graduation. Still, the voice had

Portrait of Barter's founder as a young actor—nattily dressed and on the lookout for good roles.
(Photo courtesy of Mrs. Mary Dudley Porterfield)

been untested. A little later he landed a part in Atlantic City in a play about Benvenuto Cellini. His first spoken line as a professional actor would be, "Have you seen Cellini?"

He heard his cue, strode on stage and said in his thickest Southern drawl, "Have y'all seen Cellini?" The audience roared and Bob had a story to repeat to four decades of actors.

"After acting as usher, reading to blind people, and doing many other varied chores," he once commented, "I managed to finance my theatrical education and lose my Southern accent. Since that time, I have needed my accent in every part I have played!"

Porterfield now thrust himself into the erratic lifestyle of a young struggling actor in New York. In addition to some modeling and radio work, he landed a job at the New York Athletic Club collecting tips as the front elevator boy. Among the people to drop coins in his hand were John D. Rockefeller, Mayor

Jimmy Walker and Charles Lindbergh. Gradually, he worked his way up to desk clerk, then to dining room supervisor. Parts in shows came off and on between 1927 and 1932. There was a role in *The Ivory Door* which opened at the Charles Hopkins Theatre on October 18, 1927, and bit parts in *Mima* (1928) at the Belasco Theatre, *The Dagger and the Rose* (1929), *The Blue Ghost* (1930) at the Forrest Theatre, and *Blind Windows* (1931).

Like so many others before and after him, Bob was paying his dues. At one point, everything of value was stolen from his New York apartment and he had to stay with two friends for a while.

But, also like most people who wander into the acting profession, Bob believed and, in 1932, Walter Hampden selected him to play a cadet for the *Cyrano de Bergerac* tour which resulted in the "barter" inspiration.

In a fascinating autobiographical sketch requested for the January, 1938 *Record of the Hampden-Sydney Alumni Association*, Bob jotted down some early memories of his childhood, college days and starting years as an actor:

> I was born in Wythe County (Va.) on the other side of New River. My first conscious moment was Pop in a rowboat paddlin' me and Ma across the river—the river was up and the creek was rising and they were taking me to my baptizing. Then we moved up to the Salt works, Virginia, where I was reared and fed. I was always under the belief that Saltville was the end of the world because the train turned around there on a turntable and went back to Glade Springs.
>
> My first ventures out of the "holler" were on a number of football trips in which I suffered a knee and head injuries and haven't been right since; consequently, I turned to oratory and won the ninth district oratorical contest on "The Constitution." This prompted a trip to Richmond under the sponsorship of a Richmond newspaper. I recall I slept with my britches on because I couldn't stand to take them off.
>
> On this trip I remember passing through Farmville and making a rear platform appearance (not to make a speech). I heard these words, "You have done it before, you can do it some more, Hampden-Sydney." The tune kindered my imagination and I inquired about Hampden-Sydney, as I was finishing high school that year and realized that I should seek a bit of higher education. Recalling that tune and being somewhat of a fatalist, I matriculated and my abode was "Stagger Inn." Due to weak knees, I turned to the Jangleurs and, thanks to Dr. Bell, I got my first dramatic start as William Sylvanius Baxter, Esq. in Booth Tarkington's *Seventeen*. Dr. Bell and some of my Kappa Alpha brothers encouraged me in my thespian aspirations and the combination of that encouragement and my parental objections to the theater decided me to try my luck on the stage.
>
> Upon my arrival in New York, I was rather lucky, having done shows with David Belasco, a national tour with Walter Hampden in *Cyrano de Bergerac*, a number of other Broadway shows and radio.

Just before Bob had gone to New York, his father took the family to the Porterfield farm near Glade Spring, Twin Oaks. Settled before the Revolution about 15 miles north of Abingdon, the land, as Bob was fond of saying, had been owned by only Indians and Porterfields. The stately Twin Oaks family house, like the Oprey House that housed Barter and the Martha Washington Inn that housed his first company, was also built in the early 1830s.

Of all the converts Bob made to theater during his lifetime, one held a special significance. During an illness just before his death, Bob's father rejected the prejudices ingrained by his upbringing. "Actors are about the nicest people I know," he told his son.

Chapter Four: Ham for Hamlet...Cabbage for Cash

For whatever reason—fate, chance, luck, genius, industry, timing, perseverance, inspiration, or, most likely, a combination of all these—the Barter Theatre survived 1933. The company grew to 28 and the season was expanded from seven to ten plays in 1934. Only three members of the original crew rejoined Bob and Fritchie for a second summer in Abingdon: publicity director Austin, Agnes Ives and Emily Woodruff.

To help insure Barter's future, Bob brought in young Hume Cronyn as a production director for that second year.

"I was his partner during the second season of the enterprise," Cronyn recalled. "It was still singularly his own dream and vision. I recruited two or three people who came to the company that season, and between us we managed to raise a little money for Barter. That was hard to come by back then, but a very little went a long way. I had met Bob in New York and was immediately struck by his enormous personal charm and enthusiasm. He was a natural political figure who knew how to persuade. He was better at that than almost anything."

"It was still 35 cents or the equivalent in barter at that time. We got mostly vegetables...occasionally a pig. We ate most of it. And we didn't sleep a whole lot. We really worked our asses off. And sometimes it wasn't easy to deliver on the promises he made. We used to call him 'Massah.' Bob was unbeatable at encouraging people—a very hale, easygoing, big man. To me, in 1934, it was a job. After leaving Barter I became involved rather quickly with productions in New York. One of the members of the company that year was Emily Woodruff, who later became Mrs. Hume Cronyn." (Cronyn, of course, is now married to actress Jessica Tandy, with whom he has often starred on Broadway.)

Cronyn, like most anyone who has worked at Barter, has stories to tell. Everyone seems to have their favorite Barter story. And no one was better at spinning a tale than Mr. P.

There was the farmer who led a cow to the front of the theater.

"How much milk must I pay to get in?" he asked.

"About two quarts," the ticket seller replied.

Lifting his pail, the farmer went to work until he had the necessary amount. He was about to enter the theater when the box office attendant noticed his wife standing by the cow.

"Aren't you taking your wife with you?"

"Let 'er milk her own ticket," replied the farmer indignantly.

Then there was the mountaineer who offered to pay "with something I make, only I don't think you'll want it."

The "barter" is already piled high for this matinee that was probably during the 1937 season. The building pictured is one of the Stonewall Jackson Institute structures and now houses the company's rehearsal hall.
(Photo courtesy of the Barter Theatre)

"Sure we do," cajoled the affable ticket seller.

"I make coffins," he said.

The ticket seller was stumped until the old man added that he also made canes. The coffin maker came back again and again, until every member of the Barter company had a finely carved walking stick. Bob passed out many of these canes to his friends on Broadway, later boasting they had supported many of the theater's best known actors.

A pig, admission for eight people, got loose one night and ran through the streets of Abingdon with actors in hot pursuit. They never caught it.

One small boy brought a jar of apple butter to the box office. The tasty looking delicacy turned out to be mud. A lamb used as admission was bleating so loud that it had to be quieted with milk turned in that same night as barter. Turtles bartered for tickets got loose in the lobby and scared some elderly ladies.

In addition to food, early items of barter included wine, toothpaste, snakes, livestock, and even underwear.

Another time there was a farmer who pulled up to the theater with a truck loaded with children. Marching up to the box office with a calf on a rope, he said he'd like to trade the animal for season tickets for his family. When told the calf would be enough, he asked, "You don't need nothin' else?"

As soon as the answer came back negative, he untied the calf saying, "Then you don't need the rope." Sure enough, the calf bolted, but this time a member of the company was fast enough to catch it before a chase delayed curtain time.

During the very early years, the city jail was in the basement of the theater. Inmates often got rowdy, interrupting performances.

Bob loved these stories and he repeated, embellished and enriched them for reporters and audiences year in and year out.

"You can almost tell just who is in the house any night by looking over the box office," he once said only half-jokingly.

By 1939, Porterfield and his performers had been featured on both the Fred Allen and Rudy Vallee radio shows. The wry Allen asked his listeners how the Barter box office made change. When a man plunked down a turkey, did he get a rabbit and a bunch of carrots in change? "In tomato season," he quipped, "the whole company had acidosis."

"If Porterfield wants to know if he's had a success," the nasal-voiced comedian continued, "long about Labor Day he just weighs the actors."

When the comedy team of Olsen and Johnson accepted a live chicken as admission for their long-running Broadway comedy, *Hellzapoppin'*, one columnist jokingly wrote that Porterfield was considering suing for infringement of copywright.

Even Barter's custom of using a ham as royalties was good for an often repeated story. Although such diverse playwrights as Noel Coward, Philip Barry, George Kelly, Maxwell Anderson and Thornton Wilder had gone along with this novelty, George Bernard Shaw demurred.

When the Barter staged *Candide* in 1936, the renowned British playwright

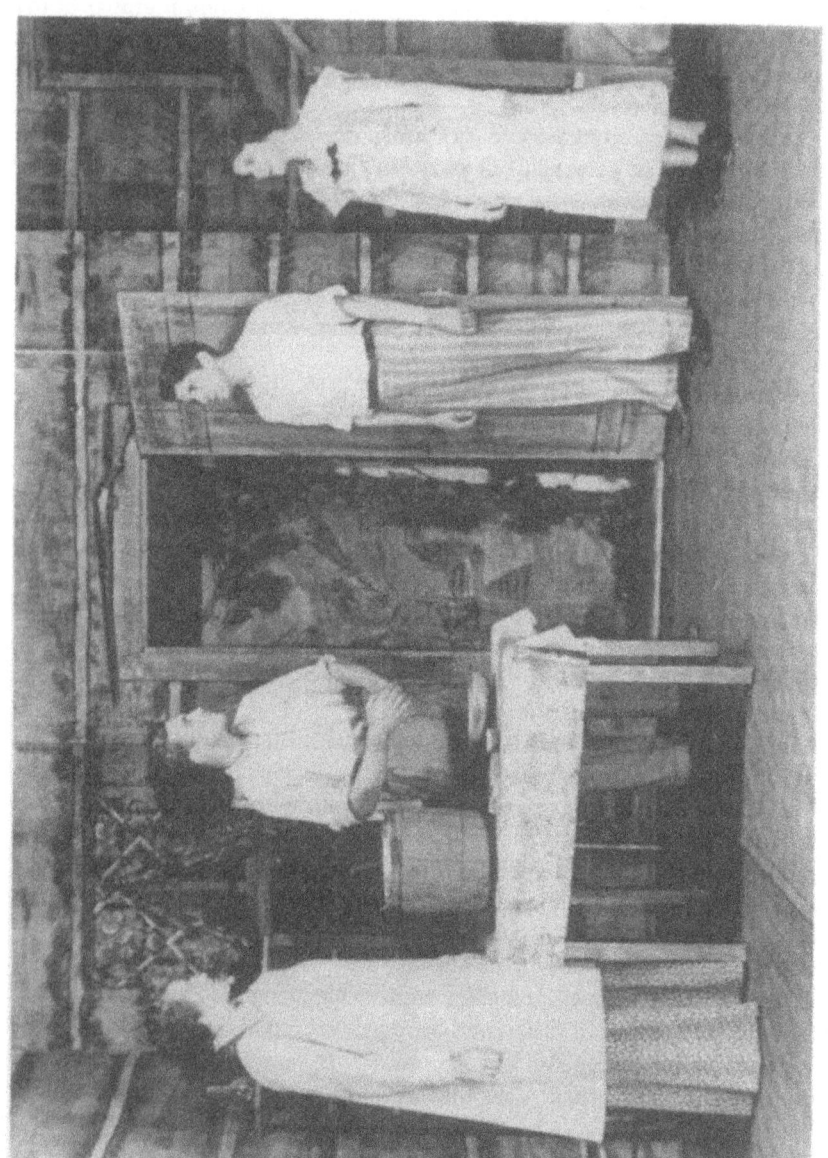

Porterfield as he appeared in a '30s production of **The Hill Between.**
(Photo courtesy of the Barter Theatre)

sent back his ham with the short explanation: "I'm a vegetarian." Three years later when the Barter wished to produce *Pygmalion*, Shaw was ready for them: "Spinach would be acceptable," he wrote.

A favorite Porterfield story was the time he compared techniques for curing hams with John Barrymore. Impressed with the Great Profile's expertise, Porterfield complimented his thorough knowledge of hams.

"I should know," Barrymore cracked. "I'm the greatest."

Bob never did totally abandon his acting career and for several years after Barter's first season he appeared on Broadway during the winter months. While Fritchie was often taking care of things in Abingdon, her husband managed to rack up a string of impressive and most prestigious credits, the most outstanding of which was the cowboy, Herb, in Robert E. Sherwood's *The Petrified Forest*.

He may have never gotten the part if it wasn't for the celebrated Porterfield charm. At first rejected for the role, he promised producer Arthur Hopkins one of the hams turned in at the Barter box office. On the way over to Hopkins' apartment with the ham, one of New York's finest stopped Porterfield and made him unwrap his rather suspicious looking package. Hopkins was so tickled by the story that he cast Porterfield opposite Leslie Howard and Humphrey Bogart.

The following year, 1936, found Bob at the Ambassador Theatre in something called *Stark Mad* by Lynn Root and Frank Fenton. Also in the cast were Tom Ewell and Percy Kilbride, so loved for his portrayal of Pa Kettle in several films with Marjorie Main. *Stark Mad* closed quickly due to bad reviews and Kilbride sent Bob the following note: "Let's pray that your next role will be more worthy of your steel." It was.

In November of the same year he was in the cast of E.P. Conkle's *Two Hundred Were Chosen*, described by *New York Times* critic Brooks Atkinson as a superlative "saga of life and death." An added measure of fame was bestowed when Porterfield and fellow cast member Will Geer were paired for a cartoon in the *Herald-Tribune*. The delightful sketch by H.H. Knight was also used on leaflets advertising the production.

Another of Broadway's leading critics, famed humorist Robert Benchley, wrote of *Two Hundred Were Chosen*: "The actors accomplish one of the minor miracles of the theater. It turns out to be one of the most interesting plays in town and one of the best acted."

Bob could also be spotted in a variety of roles in such plays as *Let Freedom Ring, The Hill Between, Bury the Dead, Everywhere I Roam, They Shall Not Die* and *John Brown*. Before turning all his attentions to Barter, Bob had appeared in some fourteen Broadway shows.

In later years, Bob preferred to tell stories about Barter more than Broadway, but when a fellow named Clark Gable became the "king" of Hollywood, he couldn't resist recalling 1931 for a Knoxville newspaperman—"Gable certainly has changed a lot since we played together in *Blind Windows*. He has a new set of teeth and his ears have been clipped."

These regular forays to New York kept Bob's perspective on an ever-changing theater world fresh and continued to make him countless invaluable friends. On a more practical level, they kept Bob's "hand in." Barter, although successful, was hardly a sure thing. There were no guarantees that his company would be back next year during the '30s.

The adventuresome Mr. P also tried his hand in Hollywood, making his film debut in the now rarely seen *The Deep South* in 1937. Actually, Bob's screen credits are also impressive, even if the roles were little more than cameos. Ultimately, many of Bob's friends and former employees ended up in California, so visits to the West Coast sometimes were coupled with experience before the camera. There was an appearance in Mervyn LeRoy's excellent 1937 drama starring Claude Rains, *They Won't Forget*; a memorable performance as Gary Cooper's rival in romance, Zeb Andrews, in *Sergeant York* (1941); *Army Chaplain* (1942); a bit part in *The Yearling* (1946), which starred Barter graduate Gregory Peck; and another small character part in Robert Mitchum's granddaddy of car-chase pictures, *Thunder Road* (1958), which was partly filmed on location in Southwest Virginia and North Carolina.

Hollywood didn't change Bob's homespun nature, of course. When he showed up in the office of a studio executive to sign for *The Yearling*, he was asked who his agent was.

"Peck," Porterfield replied plainly.

"Peck?!" the MGM executive roared. "Peck's the star."

"I know, I know. But he's my agent." And so he was. Bob could always count on his friends.

Back in Abingdon, Barter's situation was constantly changing. An apprentice program was inaugurated for the third season, and a six-day Drama Festival added to each season, with several plays offered in repertory. But perhaps the most important change occured in 1935 when a motion picture distribution chain leased the Main Street Opera House. Barter had been designated unfair competition, and Bob looked into the still vacant Stonewall Jackson campus as an alternate site. Although not centrally located, these facilities—including a 500-seat auditorium—were available for a modest rent, so Bob and company said a temporary goodbye to the Oprey House and Martha Washington Inn. After the war, Barter Theatre once again called Main Street home, this time for good, but the company residence—the old Stonewall Jackson dormitory rechristened the Barter Inn—the scene shop remained "up on the hill" at the former Stonewall Jackson Institute.

And Barter continued to make news. In 1936, Porterfield took a double bill of 16th century plays—*Everyman* and Henry Porter's *Two Angry Women of Abingdon*—to New York and staged them at Barter prices. Response to the appearance at the New School of Social Science auditorium was excellent from reviewers and audiences, and "big city" theatergoers had their chance to pay 35 cents or the equivalent in barter. Bob continued such annual New York showcase performances until the war broke out, offering three plays in three days during the 1940 trip.

Several newspapers and the wire services took notice of a bureaucratic ruling that became a Barter cause celebre. When a Barter sow had eight piglets, the AAA decreed that was one over the limit and ordered one killed. Well, that's a potential royalty the agency was so callously playing with, so the battle was joined. The debate over the "litter of eight" ended on a delightful note when no less than Chief Justice Charles Evans Hughes ruled the eighth piglet could survive. Hams of both varieties applauded the decision.

In the July 31, 1939 issue of *Life* magazine, Bob and Barter received one of their single most famous pieces of publicity. A full-page photograph titled "How to Make Love" showed a serious-minded Porterfield demonstrating the proper romantic embrace to 12 couples in earnest clinches. The hill-side panorama was repeated in "Best of *Life*" spreads and was recreated for *It's A Date*, a Universal film starring Deanna Durbin.

Barter was even the subject of a front page feature in *The London Times* (Sept. 8, 1936). Still, few honors could be counted as high as the front of the July 23, 1939 *New York Times* drama section. There, in that now legendary style, was a Hirschfeld interpretation of Bob and the Barter Theatre lobby.

A 1939 rendering of the Barter Theatre lobby for the New York Times by famed artist Hirschfeld.

Chapter Five: Mr. P

In today's world of million-dollar ad campaigns, slick network packaging, and cheap wrestling matches, the word promoter carries something of an ugly connotation. But let's assume that a promoter pushes something either worthwhile or fraudulent; his methods are either admirable or despicable. Allowing for that and the basic necessity for public relations in the arts, Bob Porterfield was a promoter in the very best sense of the word.

Barter survived four decades of change very simply because again and again, Porterfield displayed uncanny ingenuity in promoting his theater.

"Porterfield was a man of many talents," explained the man who succeeded him, Rex Partington. "He acted, directed, produced, but I think his forte was promotion."

Partington's vantage point is not to be taken lightly. He has steered the Abingdon theater through another decade of growth after Bob's death, and has kept Barter a vital, vibrant company.

"He was a promoter and a very decent one; with the spirit and guts to keep it going," Hume Cronyn stated.

One way Porterfield kept the theater in the national eye year after year was through the Barter Award. With the exception of the New York Drama Critics Circle Award, which started in 1936, there was nothing close to a gala evening that brought together the American theater's luminaries. The Pulitzer Prize, after all, was announced very dryly and the Tony Awards were not initiated until 1947. And there was that legion of carefully cultivated New York friends who would willingly help out the Barter if Porterfield asked.

So, each year Porterfield assembled old and new friends to present the Barter Theatre Award. Although his stated purpose was to recognize America's leading performers, the much-publicized New York banquet quickly became a highlight of the theatrical social season.

"The Barter Theatre has decided to present an award to the American who has given the most outstanding performance on the stage in the current year," wrote First Lady Eleanor Roosevelt in her syndicated column, *My Day*. "The first recipient of this award is Miss Laurette Taylor, and they accorded me the honor of presenting her with it."

Mrs. Roosevelt was already on record as a friend of Barter. As far back as 1936 she had expressed interest in Bob Porterfield's experiment, possibly because her father had lived in Abingdon for a number of years. The *New York Journal* recorded the following White House conversation between the First Lady and a Washington County resident:

Ethel Barrymore, considered the "First Lady" of the American theater, won the third Barter Award in 1941, and received the traditional ham and an acre of land from First Lady Eleanor Roosevelt. Present at the award ceremonies were, left to right, Porterfield, Mrs. Roosevelt, Barrymore, Laurette Taylor (first Barter Award winner), and Dorothy Stickney (1940 winner).
(Photo courtesy of the Barter Theatre)

"Do you know about the Barter Theatre?" Mrs Roosevelt inquired.

"Yes, I surely do," the Abingdon woman replied.

"Do, you know about the young man who has charge of the theater?"

"Yes, I know him. He is Robert Porterfield, a native of Washington County and we are very proud of him."

It would be the first of many times the popular First Lady would vocally lend her support to Bob's theater.

The first Barter Award was bestowed at a New York luncheon, with Porterfield acting as master of ceremonies. Laurette Taylor, already a Broadway legend, but an actress with many great performances ahead, was chosen for her portrayal of the charwoman in *Outward Bound*. With the exception of the guests of honor, everyone paid for their own meals—and those in attendance included Helen Hayes, Tallulah Bankhead, Sophie Tucker, Robert Morely and Marc Connelly.

Of course, there remained a distinct Southwest Virginia flavor to the proceedings: the award consisted of a Virginia ham and an acre of land in Barter territory. Oh yes, and a special platter bearing the Barter emblem by the Cumbow China Decorating Company of Abingdon to eat that ham off of. In addition, each year's winner selected two promising performers to spend a summer in Abingdon. Taylor chose Larry Gates and Edith Sommer.

The next year, Dorothy Stickney picked Gregory Peck and Evelyn Wells Fargo. From 1939 until 1969, when the presentations stopped, Virginia hams were bestowed on such stars as Ethel Barrymore, Mildred Natwick, Helen Hayes, Henry Fonda, Tallulah Bankhead, Shirley Booth, Frederic March, Rosalind Russell, David Wayne, Mary Martin, Julie Harris, Ethel Merman, George Abbott, Abe Burrows, David Merrick, Robert Preston and Pearl Bailey.

Few awards can boast such an impressive selection of recipients. And, predictably, it was good for more than its share of stories. Perhaps the most publicized moment came in 1954 when David Wayne won the Barter Award. A ban by the Stage Hands Union—probably incurred because Porterfield didn't use union stage hands at the Barter—forced 137 hopeful actors into the alley beside the Martin Beck Theatre. Undaunted, Wayne, with the help of former Barter actor Larry Gates, conducted auditions under the fire escape. A picture of these unique tryouts was widely circulated.

Ethel Barrymore, the grande dame of the American theater, allowed each performer only one minute for the 1941 auditions. There were about 400 that year, and when asked to explain her method, she commented wryly, "If they have talent, you'll know it. If they don't, you'll think your watch has stopped."

When not busy in Abingdon, New York or Hollywood, Porterfield was a popular lecturer at luncheons, civic functions, club meetings, seminars and workshops. A natural platform performer, Bob would loosen up his audience with a few Barter stories before completely winning them over with his charm, wit and genuine concern for the survival of live theater in America. To state and local officials he constantly stressed Barter's capacity to attract tourists and out-

The 1954 Barter Award went to David Wayne who chose Paul Lukather, left, and Phyllis Wynn to spend a season in Abingdon.
(Photo courtesy of the Barter Theatre)

of-state revenue. To students and educators he was unflinching in his dedication to quality theater.

"He encouraged schools and other theaters all the time," pointed out Owen Phillips, Bob's close friend and frequent Barter director. "He always said good theater helps us all. Bad theater hurts everybody."

"I spend a great deal of time discouraging young people from going into theater," Porterfield once said. "It's a demanding profession in which there's virtually no home life, an abundance of long and often irregular hours, and plenty of headaches and heartaches. Anyone who can be discouraged should be and will be discouraged."

But that didn't mean students shouldn't be exposed to the dramatic process. And if it was going to be of any benefit at all, Bob argued, it should be with capable instructors and proper facilities.

"What we need are more stages and more audiences to accomodate all of the dedicated young actors and actresses on their way up."

On another occasion he remarked, "Student dramatics never will be as good

Governor Tuck of Virginia joins Robert Porterfield in honoring Barter Award winner Talullah Bankhead.
(Photo courtesy of the Barter Theatre)

as they should until schools put them on purely for artistic purposes, not to raise money for new gym equipment."

Undeniably, Bob's vision was never restricted to his own theater. He was constantly promoting theater as a vital and necessary part of people's lives. He never stopped looking into new ways he and his theater could enrich his town, region, state and country.

An outgrowth of that deep concern and his brilliance for promotion naturally led him towards a proposal that was coming into focus about the same time as the Barter Award. By 1940, Porterfield was writing and spending a lot of time with Virginia legislators, campaigning for his latest brainstorm: "My dream is to have the first state theater in the Commonwealth of Virginia. Wouldn't it be grand if we had 48 state theaters? Then we *would* have a national theater."

He had originally worked up a proposal for a federally subsidized program in 1935—an early effort at strength through decentralization. If President Roosevelt, Relief Administrator Harry Hopkins, and two Virginia senators were not impressed, the people who heard Bob push his "state theaters" plan in personal appearances were.

And several elected officials had their ears bent by a relentless Porterfield in 1940, who was in Richmond working for the state Department of Education on a drama-in-schools project. By September, he had the particulars of his plan worked out. If the federal government wasn't going to take the initiative, well, he hoped his new venture in Richmond "may some day set a national precedent by becoming the first American state theater."

"My goal is to establish a professional festival-resident company that will tour the state during the fall, winter and spring as an 'Exhibit A' for the colleges and schools to observe. I expect eventually to pick, with the aid of a competent committee of Virginians acquainted with the theater, three plays out of the 15 we will experiment with during the summer season at Abingdon. Then we'll move our base to one of the college towns and play each night for a five-week period in a radius of 60 miles."

"During the daytime, a part of the professional actors will rehearse with the college students towards a major production at the end of the fifth week. The remainder, in the mean time, will direct productions in elementary and high schools in that area. After five weeks in one location, we will move to another college town for the same length of time, permitting in all about five festival sessions over the state."

Porterfield was a hard man to resist and unexpected help came once again from Mrs. Roosevelt, who wrote in *My Day*: "It is exciting to have a state government finally realize the importance of the theater in the life of the people."

The war, however, interfered with Bob's plans. The second World War saw 135 former Barter players in the armed forces. Four won the Distinguished Service Cross. Two gave their lives.

The Barter was closed for the duration and its founder found himself in the Air Force. Porterfield later joked that the GI who interviewed him, "refused his

Head sticking above the rest, stage-center, Bob Porterfield poses with his cast for **Two On An Island**.
(Photo courtesy of the Barter Theatre)

request for liason work, stating that the army did not provide for illicit relationships."

But the laughter died in 1944 when a tornado swept through Abingdon. The word that reached Bob—stationed in Texas at the time—was indeed disheartening. Equipment, scenery, costumes, scripts and props had been destroyed by wind and flooding. Losses were estimated a $20,000. Barter had been devastated and even Bob had doubts about continuing.

After being discharged in 1945, Bob went to Hollywood. It was writer James Hilton who provided the incentive for Porterfield's return to Abingdon. The author of *Lost Horizon* and *Goodbye Mr. Chips* was yet another keen observer of Barter's growth. He personally sent actors to Barter to gain experience, and it was his wish to eventually retire to Abingdon because the quaint town reminded him so much of an English country town. Hilton never did settle in Southwest Virginia. He died in California after several successful novels and screenplays. Hilton's wife Alice, however, became Bob's secretary in the late '40s, devoting time and money to keep Barter going until her death in 1962. To this day,

Hilton's Best Screenplay Oscar for *Mrs. Miniver* sits on the Barter Inn desk of business manager Pearl Hayter.

Hilton told Bob that in Hollywood he would be just one among thousands and thousands of actors. But in Virginia he could still make an important contribution to the American theater.

Faith renewed, Bob got to work. It turned out that the Abingdon Town Council wanted Barter back very badly. The Opera House was again reserved for Barter's use, and with what Bob and friends were able to raise, repairs were effected.

Porterfield once again went before the Virginia Legislature and this time he got what he wanted. It didn't set a national precedent as Bob hoped, but when Barter reopened its doors in 1946, it was boosted by $10,000 in state funding and in title, "The State Theatre of Virginia."

Today, Barter's support from the state comes in the form of a four-to-one matching grant. For every $4 the Barter raises (1981 figures), the state kicks in $1 up to a $50,000 annual limit.

Although a great tribute to Bob's idealism and far-sighted beliefs, the "State Theatre" designation was also his greatest single piece of promotion. Without it, Barter may not have survived to celebrate a 50th anniversary.

The post-war period saw other very necessary changes. A season ticket campaign was initiated; actors were put on salary; and a cash box office replaced the beloved Barter system.

"That was the change that created the most trouble," Barter historian Dr. Anne St. Clair Williams noted. "There were a lot of people who were faithful Barter patrons who had never used anything but vegetables to see a show. One of the most vocal was a black woman who ran the fish market in Abingdon. There was another woman who had planted an extra row of beans to use as barter when she heard the theater was going to reopen. How could you explain the economic necessity of a cash box office to such loyal patrons? The reaction was so strong that Bob let some people still use barter—but only in Abingdon."

Bob also investigated and experimented with ways to promote Abingdon as a tourist attraction. One of his brainstorms was the Virginia Highlands Festival, which remains a leading showcase for arts and crafts. Each August finds a huge big-top tent set up on the lawn across from Barter and between the Barter Playhouse and the Martha Washington Inn. The fair's popularity has brought valuable tourist revenue to Abingdon and, not suprisingly, some of Barter's best houses.

Part of being a good promoter means keeping the customer satisfied, and Bob was always acutely aware of the image his theater projected in Abingdon. From the moment he walked his company to church in 1933, Mr. P made it abundantly clear that his actors could ill afford to alienate the community.

"At first," Porterfield recalled, "the Abingdon people were suspicious of the actors as an evil influence, but they were soon won over. The Barter Theatre has never had a scandal."

A post-war Barter company prepares to leave for another touring engagement.
(Photo courtesy of The Barter Theatre)

"They were a little dubious at first," he remarked on another occasion. "However, they need not have any qualms. I had made it clearly understood nobody was going to indulge in any mid-summer orgies. Hard work, rather than dissipation, was to be the rule of the day. We felt our way cautiously and gave mostly simple little productions, going strong on broad comedy in that first season. We don't think that the type of patron we were appealing to would care for heavy drama or sophistication. Today, however, there has been a marked expansion of taste and we now receive little criticism when we offer plays that would have been considered daring beyond words back in 1932."

Lou Flanigan, a stage manager at Barter in the late '60s and now the theater's public relations director, remembers walking with Bob Porterfield through Abingdon and being amazed by his easy manner as he passed people on the street. "He was very community conscious and he made sure the theater projected a proper image. Part of that meant cultivating the community."

A "free thinker, an individualist, an independent speaker, a 'spinner of yarns,' 'the man on the street,' and the man next door all rolled into one dynamic person." That's how one local journalist described Robert Porterfield. Barter's survival simply can not be explained without understanding what formidable gifts and characteristics its founder possessed.

"It wasn't promoting in the way we think of it," actress Cleo Holladay declares today. "It was a natural charm. He could sell anything." Holladay, who is now married to Barter producing director Rex Partington, was chosen by Mary Martin in 1955 as a Barter Award winner. "Right away Bob made you feel like you were part of the theater. He had enormous sensitivity for both his actors and the town of Abingdon."

Charm. Few people can recall Bob Porterfield without using that word over and over. Certainly Bob's distinct ability for promotion was a major factor in the Barter's survival, but, hand in hand with that talent was the man's overwhelming charm.

"I'm sure there were some people who didn't find him charming," commented Frank Lowe, an actor in the Barter company for much of the '50s. "Anyone without enemies is suspect. But most found him hard to resist. Barter was the least likely spot in the world for a professional theater. It's still isolated, but when he started it, Barter was extremely isolated. He had the uncanny ability to encourage people to come to the theater. They were difficult audiences in that they wouldn't stand for anything bad.

"Bob had a very intuitive nature. There were constant changes in the American theater, Abingdon, the country and the world; and Barter reflected that. And Barter was a place where lifelong friendships were made. It was a hard existence, but very instructive. Bob wasn't a remote boss. He was very helpful, supportive and he dealt with you on an intensely personal level. I found him an uncommonly trusting man if he had faith in you. But he liked to see people get out of their own problems. If he thought you were wrong, but you honestly believed in what you were doing, he'd let you do it. If he thought you'd learn something, he'd let you fall flat on your face.

"Once when I was in the hospital in New York, I was quite ill and very low. Who should walk in but Bob Porterfield and he said, 'You've got to get out of here and go to work down in Abingdon'."

"He was not bound by greed...a singular producer. He had a professional charm that he used as an actor—he knew how to play an audience—and a separate charm that was his own personality. He was rather a religious man, yet very open-minded. He was interested in a lot of things."

The memories of friends and associates bear out Barter scholar Teresa Keller's assertion that Bob "has been deified." Consider just a few of these cherished recollections:

Ann Buckles was an actress in the Barter company in 1951, returning to play the lead in the 1971 production of *40 Carats* just a few months before Bob's death: "Bob Porterfield was certainly a guiding force for me. He saw a creative spark and encouraged it. And when I went to New York that fall ('51), Bob sent a whole folder of letters to influential people for me. Years later, whenever I saw him in New York, he'd say, 'When you coming to Abingdon to do a show?' "

"He was a generous person. He truly loved the theater, and the area. I remember one night we were partying quite loudly at the Barter Inn. All of a sudden there was a knock on the door and there stood Bob. He just looked at me with a steady stare and then said simply, 'Blondes dissipate faster than brunettes,' and walked away,' " leaving his blonde actress open-mouthed and with no good comeback.

Cathy DeCaterina is the founder of Theatre Bristol, a respected community theater nearby. Bob came to see a couple of her early children's productions, but her favorite Porterfield memory harkens back to when she was a student at Juilliard in New York: "One day I ran into Bob Porterfield on the street. It was so wonderful to see this warm face from home and I just smiled and said, 'Hi, Mr Porterfield.' Well, his face just lit up and he treated me like I was a long-lost relative. I was naive enough to think he actually remembered my name and he was just nice enough to let me think I was like a first cousin."

Lynn Pecktal was a Kingsport native attending Emory and Henry College just a few miles away from Abingdon when he was tapped by Porterfield to be the company's set designer in 1955. Working during the summers while finishing his degree, Pecktal went on to spend nine consecutive seasons at Barter—returning for a stint in 1966 and a special assignment in 1981 and 1982—designing sets for such varied shows as *Cat On a Hot Tin Roof*, *The Waltz of the Toreadors* and *Teahouse of the August Moon*. Like many others who worked at Barter, Pecktal got more than just a promising career start in Abingdon, since it was during his first season that he met Georgia Bennett, the actress who five years later became his wife and the mother of their two sons. He is now recognized as a leading authority on set design and his 1975 text book, *Designing for the Theater*, is considered the definitive work on the subject. Scenic design is a difficult field to break into and the Barter gave Pecktal a chance to create many diverse types of sets before he established himself in New York. An imposing oil painting of his set for Tennessee Williams' *Cat On a Hot Tin Roof*—which featured Ned Beatty as Big Daddy—still hangs in the first floor hallway of the Barter Inn.

"This was a proving ground," Pecktal stated. "It was a great place to learn. Robert Porterfield was a great, driving force for young people and demanded the best. In those days, we were doing shows on very tight budgets. You had to use your imagination and be as resourceful as possible. I can remember closing a show on a Sunday night and opening on a Monday...or building several sets at once."

"Bob never let you down, though, when you needed something. You could ask him for anything, and, as long as you could justify the expense, you'd get it. He had a marvelous intuitive sense about productions. When he didn't want to spend money on a set, all I had to do was say to Mr. P, 'Okay, if you want it to look tacky.' "

"Eventually, the time came to move on. Bob tried to get me to stay but he understood. There was never any clash between friendship and professionalism with Bob. I thought the world of him as did many people."

Bob Gallico, who now makes his home in Ireland, came to Barter as an aspiring actor in the early '50s. The son of writer Paul Gallico, his memories of Barter are both wistful and vivid: "The one thing I must say is that there is something very special about the Barter Theatre. Actors work in summer stock and repertory theaters all over, but they always remember the Barter Theatre. That's partly due to Robert Porterfield. He was a helluva character in his own right. He was a charmer, a showman, a promoter—but he demanded the best."

"The Barter was the best training an actor could have. We played in a library one night, an airplane hangar the next. And all the classic things happened—sets fell down, door handles fell off. It was probably less professional than some theaters, but it was a lot more exciting. You know, friendships, marriages and romances started at Barter because of the atmosphere. There was a sense of identity and family; and Bob was very much a father figure. He could be cruel and kind and gentle and wise and generous. Bob and Barter represent the best of theater. Actors are transitory beings, but the Barter is something that they always remember. Even if I had never come back to Abingdon, I would never forget it."

Nancy Necessary Pridemore has been a speech and drama teacher at Kingsport's Dobyns-Bennett High School for some 35 years: "I knew Bob Porterfield really well and was able to get a lot of students apprenticeships at the Barter. I remember going to see Barter productions on 'Barter'—we all took garden vegetables. As children, we thought it was so exciting. We didn't know what Barter was all about because there was no live theater in this area up to that point. Bob's influence in this area is tremendous. They've kept theater alive and they've definitely inspired other theater groups. Countless children were introduced to the magic of live theater through Barter. They've helped this area grow culturally. There's no way to fully appreciate what Barter has accomplished. And Bob was so tall, and handsome, and square-shouldered. He had great stage presence."

Anne St. Clair Williams worked closely with Porterfield in developing her 1967 thesis research. She said of him, "He didn't need a character to hide behind, because he was a character."

In ill health for several years, Bob's beloved Fritchie died in 1949. Before the war, the first Mrs. Porterfield was responsible in large part for Barter's financial survival. Bob always needed that one person to "watch the pennies." Alice Hilton filled that function for some years, with Pearl Price Hayter, a Barter employee since the '50s, succeeding her. Fiercely loyal to Bob and Rex Partington, Barter's current business manager is an integral part of the theater's history and future.

"Amazing charm," is the way Pearl sums up Mr. P. "That's how he got so much accomplished. He has become something of a saint since his death, but I don't think that's the way he'd want to be remembered. He was very human and he was well aware of it. He knew theater. He knew talent. He knew how to persuade. He wasn't a great businessman and he was a great one for promising things without being sure he could deliver on it or not. He was extremely careful about the actors socializing with the community. Bob ran a happy ship but he also believed in discipline."

Pearl, of course, is quite accurate. As with many men of charisma, a myth has grown up around Bob Porterfield. When Abingdon residents and former Barter actors remember Bob, there is a reverence and affection in their tone. Granted, this is more than deserved, yet it keeps us from getting a complete personal picture of Bob. What was he like at home? What kind of person impressed him? What were his politics? What were his peculiar characteristics?

When Bob talked to the press it was generally about Barter; rarely about himself. Once or twice, some intimate hints came out.

"I like authentic folk music and the folk ballad," he said in 1954, "but I never have been very much on this popular stuff."

Was he a prude? Well, he certainly had a great deal of "Old South" morality to him. A man should be a gentleman no matter what his station in life and a woman should be a Lady with a capital 'L.' He didn't approve of cursing, particularly in front of a woman. The virtues of the "Protestant Work Ethic" wasn't lost on him, either.

Still, Bob apparently was open to new ideas.

"At times there are plays presented which are called shady and dirty and immoral," he stated in 1947. "We don't want to give such performances. With the people in support of the theater, they can demand plays that are significant and carry a worthy message along with their entertainment. The future is up to them."

The person best able to fill in some of these gray areas is Mary Dudley Porterfield, the gracious Lady (with a capital 'L') who Bob married in 1965. She still lives on the Twin Oaks farm in a home filled with memories of Bob. It's about time Mary Dudley had center stage:

"He always said, 'if you're not doing something you like, you won't make a success of it.' He had fun. I still think he was one of the greatest promoters in the American theater, and not just because he was my husband. I had worked for Barter once and he asked me to come back and organize the Friends of Barter (an organization of community supporters). That's when it all started. He lived at the Barter Inn at the time and we were married and he moved back to Twin Oaks permanently. It's always been a Grade-A dairy. He adored this place."

"Let's see. He hated smoking; hated hairspray; hated drunkenness. Loved his women to smell sweet. He used to say, 'I married Mary Dudley because she smells like perfume and not linament.' He hated people who pretended. He was very considerate and thoughtful of people. The only time I saw him get really mad was at Actors' Equity. He could get so mad at them."

"Bob had the kind of personality that you felt when he came into a room. You just had a good time when you were around Bob. You never knew what he

Bob Porterfield and his beloved mother, Miss Daisy, share a quiet moment beneath the Twin Oaks for which the Porterfield homestead is named.
(Photo courtesy of Mrs. Mary Dudley Porterfield)

was going to say. The curtain speeches were never planned."

Ah, the curtain speeches...so much a part of Barter's lore. It is a tradition maintained by Partington. Bob would use that folksy charm before each show. From 1947 on, he gave away a pair of nylon stockings to the person attending a Barter performance for the first time from the farthest distance away.

"Anyone here from Asia, Africa, Isaiah," he'd start.

Too often, he'd get rolling and just keep going, sending the actors into agonizing fits behind the curtain. He always ended his curtain speech with the same piece of advice: "If ya' like us, talk about us. If ya' don't, jes keep ya' mouth shut!"

"That's when he put them in his pocket," Fritz Weaver maintained.

"The guy ate audiences," Anne St. Clair Williams concurred.

"The actors used to tease him or pull his coat through the curtain when he went on," Mary Dudley remembered with a chuckle. "His mind was working all the time. When he found out that Lady Bird Johnson was on a beautification tour, he got on the phone and invited her to a performance. And he got her. He was a perfectionist...always striving."

"You couldn't take a bad picture of Bob. He was the most photogenic person in the world. He was perfectly happy in old work clothes or a tuxedo. He adored dressing up, but he looked good in anything."

"There was no place you could go where he didn't know somebody or he wasn't recognized. We took a year off and went to Europe and there wasn't anyplace we went where people didn't know about Barter. When we went to any kind of function, we never sat together. We always sat at separate tables. My job was public relations. That way we could reach twice as many people. He never stopped promoting. He kept a pencil and notebook by his bed and he'd wake up and write down ideas."

"He collected little animals and little pocket books, but his real hobby was the theater and Twin Oaks. He liked fishing, but he wasn't a big sportsman. He couldn't stand to waste time. He was a big reader, constantly reading anything concerned with theater and plays. *Variety* was his Bible. Bob seemed to know a little about everything."

"He was a Democrat, but he wasn't politically active. He knew that both Democrats and Republicans were coming to his theater."

"He was a frugal man. He knew what the Depression was and what breadlines were. I remember our first Christmas here at Twin Oaks, I had prepared a turkey. Well, we used that damn turkey every way I could think of—meals, leftovers, sandwiches, you name it. When there was nothing left but the bones, I gathered them up and took them out back to throw in the field. All of a sudden I was aware of this long shadow in front of me. 'What are you doing,' Bob said. When I told him I was throwing out the bones, he said, 'Boil them and make soup."

"He was a regular movie-goer. He loved *Gone With the Wind*. We never went anywhere that we didn't go to a theater. Bob also loved television. He could watch anything, but he got real excited when he'd see something with one of his Barter people in it."

"He was a good cook, a good dancer, and a good bridge player. He also loved hats. It didn't matter what kind."

"He had a Southern drawl in his voice, but it wasn't a strong accent. He had a little crack in his voice—it was so appealing. He didn't realize he had it. It was a very pleasing voice. It's hard to describe. It was intriguing."

"Groundhog Day was his biggest day. He gave a lot of attention to his Groundhog Day Letters. He said, 'I only send Groundhog Day Letters to people who sent me Christmas cards.' Of course, he didn't send Christmas Cards himself."

Lucky recipients cherished and saved Bob's Groundhog Day letters. They would usually begin:

GROUNDHOG DAY GREETINGS
I thought of you on
>Lincoln's Birthday
>Good Friday
>Washington's Birthday
>Memorial Day
>Independence Day
>Labor Day
>Columbus Day
>General Election Day
>Armistice Day
>Thanksgiving Day
>Christmas Day
>New Year's Day

but most especially I am thinking of you on this
GROUNDHOG DAY

"The letters were a summary of the preceding year and usually contained lighthearted greetings, witticisms, doses of philosophy; and were sent to family, friends and Barter patrons," Teresa Keller explained.

> At Stonehenge in England I really had a strange, goose-pimply feeling that I had been there before in another incarnation and I said so to Mary Dudley. When at the ruins of the House of the Vestal Virgins, Mary Dudley said "I have been here before in another incarnation." My laugh echoed through the Forum and I'm sure Caesar, Anthony and even Brutus must have smiled.
> 1966

> I hope you realize you can't take it with you, even though they are now making coffins with pockets for those who wish to try.
> 1969

There was one other side to Bob's private life that must be noted: that of loving father. In 1968, Bob and Mary Dudley were under the great twin oaks for which the Porterfield spread was named.

Bob, Mary Dudley, Jay Bird, and their Irish Wolfhound.
(Photo courtesy of Mrs. Mary Dudley Porterfield)

"I said to her," he recalled the following year, " 'Did you know there has not been a child to play under these oaks since my father was a boy in 1870. That was nigh on to 100 years ago. Let's adopt a little boy to play and live under these oaks.' We did. To think Mary Dudley and I have been married only four years and now we have a five-year old son. We named him Jay Bird Payne Porterfield. He is keeping me young. And he is aging his mother!"

There are no terms to describe how strong the bond between father and son became. One Groundhog Day Letter from 1969 noted: "We adopted Jay Bird. Once while struggling with him during a bath, I asked him if they didn't have a bath tub where he came from. He said he took a bath in a bucket. It's wonderful to get him out of that bucket."

"They adored each other, Jay and Bob," Mary Dudley remarked. "They were best friends."

At one point, Mary Dudley interrupted her narrative and apologized if she was rambling or getting overly animated. "He's my favorite subject," she explained.

She's not alone in that sentiment.

One of the best descriptions of Bob Porterfield came from distant relative, Tommy Curtin, a professional performer himself and the owner-manager of Bristol's Holiday Cinema movie theater.

"If you met him," Curtin stated with a smile, "you knew he had to be the one who started that theater...he was one of a kind."

Chapter Six: The Stars of Barter

The stocky young man and his friend were hungry, disheveled and exhausted. They had hitchhiked from Connecticut to Abingdon, Va., where they had heard, Bob Porterfield was auditioning performers for his Barter Theatre company.

It was 1946 and Ernest Borgnine, just out of the Navy, didn't know what to do with his life. As it turned out, his mother, Anna Bosselli Borgnine came up with the answer, "Ernie," she told him, "did you ever think of acting? You always enjoyed making a damned fool of yourself."

So, after a short stay at the Connecticut School of Dramatic Arts, the youngster took the road to Abington. Porterfield came down the hill from the Barter Inn to interview the two hapless looking prospects and assumed they wanted to build sets.

"I'm an actor," Borgnine protested.

Porterfield smiled and threw his hand to his neck—"I'm up to here in actors."

Soon, however, the aspiring thespian graduated from set-building and costume construction to bit parts. Nine years later, Ernie picked up the Best Actor Oscar for his moving portrayal of Paddy Chayefsky's lonely butcher, *Marty*.

Porterfield's response was typical: "We're extremely proud and happy that Ernest won the Academy Award. But we're not surprised."

Later, Borgnine would say, "I learned (to switch characters) thoroughly at Barter Theatre. I can never be grateful enough to Bob Porterfield and Barter for starting me on the way and for grounding me in all the facets of acting. It's because I was trained there in every possible sort of role that I'm able now to pick scripts and get a variety of characters....There's at least one (Barter player) in almost every picture I make and we keep running into old friends all over town."

Still later, he would add, "That's where I really learned my profession...by doing, by watching people."

His story is hardly unique. The honor roll of Barter Theatre alumni is an impressive list of New York and Hollywood's leading film, television and theater performers.

"You can go right down Broadway on any given night and find a Barter alumnus in some show," Fritz Weaver commented. Consider that since its inception in 1933, Barter has produced the likes of Hume Cronyn, Frank Lovejoy, Gregory Peck, Patricia Neal, Margaret Phillips, Larry Gates, Borgnine, Herbert Nelson, Elizabeth Wilson, Claude Akins, Weaver, David (Al) Hedison,

Ernest Borgnine, far left, in post-war Barter production of **Much Ado About Nothing**. Just learning his trade, Borgnine would walk off with Best Actor Oscar for **Marty** some ten years later. Other cast members are John Vivyan, Karl Lucas, Larry Gates, Frederic Warriner and Hank Colman (crouching). (Photo courtesy of the Barter Theatre)

Ernest Borgnine accepts his Best Actor Oscar from Grace Kelly.
(Photo courtesy of the Barter Theatre)

Grant Williams, Rosemary Murphy, Diane Cilento, Ned Beatty, Robert Pastene, Gerome Ragni, Gary Collins, Mitch Ryan, Larry Linville, David Birney, Richard Sanders and David Selby.

Consider, too, just some of their accomplishments. A complete list would fill an entire other book, but even a brief rundown is indeed staggering:

*HUME CRONYN, at Barter for the second season in 1934 as a director and actor, returning in 1938 to direct, he has become one of Broadway's most respected performers, often starring with his wife, Jessica Tandy. A versatile actor, Cronyn played Polonius to Richard Burton's *Hamlet*, and in *Richard III*,

Moliere's *The Miser*, Chekhov's *The Three Sisters* and *The Cherry Orchard*, comedies like *Room Service* and *The Male Animal*, and, memorably, with Tandy in *The Fourposter, Noel Coward in Two Keys* and *The Gin Game*. Well known for their devotion to the theater, the Cronyns will experiment with new shows, appear with repertory companies or tour with the same devotion they bring to Broadway. His forays into film include *Shadow of Doubt* (1943), *Lifeboat* (1944), *The Postman Always Rings Twice* (1946), *Brute Force* (1947), *Sunrise at Campobello* (1960), *Gaily, Gaily* (1969), *There Was a Crooked Man* (1970), *The Parallax View* (1974) and *Rollover* (1981).

*FRANK LOVEJOY, who started at Barter in 1935, went on to a successful film, stage and television career before his tragically premature death at the age of 48 of a heart attack in 1962. Under contract for Warner Bros., he appeared in *Home of the Brave* (1949), *Breakthrough* (1950), *In A Lonely Place* (1950), *Goodbye My Fancy* (1951), *House of Wax* (1953), *Strategic Air Command* (1955) and *Three Brave Men* (1957) with fellow Barterite Borgnine. Lovejoy also made numerous appearances in "live" television anthology programs, such as *Four Star Playhouse, Stage 7, Ford Star Jubilee, Rheingold Theatre, Zane Grey Theatre, Playhouse 90,* and a memorable starring role in the *Lux Video Theatre* production of *Double Indemnity*. In 1956, he replaced Ralph Bellamy in *Man Against Crime*, the TV series about hard-boiled detective Mike Barnett. The following year, he landed another series, *Meet McGraw* (1957-59), again starring as a tough guy adventurer. On Broadway, Lovejoy appeared in Gore Vidal's *The Best Man*.

*JEFFREY LYNN (GEOFFREY LIND) was one of 15 youngsters chosen for Barter's first apprentice program in 1935. He arrived at Barter as Geoffrey Lind and as unschooled as one could wish for. During his stay, he stage managed, acted and directed a one-act. Within a couple of years, Jeffrey Lynn was a rising star in Hollywood, appearing with the likes of Humphrey Bogart and James Cagney in *The Roaring Twenties* (1939), *It all Came True* (1940), *The Fighting 69th* (1940), *All This and Heaven Too* (1940), *Lost Lagoon* (1958) and *Tony Rome* (1967). Lynn also starred in the short-lived 1953 TV sit-com, *My Son Jeep*—remembered today by only the most ardent trivia experts—and hosted the dramatic anthology series, *Star Stage*, for one year.

*GREGORY PECK was selected for the company by Barter Award winner Dorothy Stickney in 1940. Triumphs in Hollywood followed quickly with *The Keys of the Kingdom* (1945), *The Yearling* (1946), *Duel in the Sun* (1947), *Gentleman's Agreement* (1947), *Twelve O'Clock High* (1949), *The Gunfighter* (1950), *Captain Horatio Hornblower* (1951), *Pork Chop Hill* (1959), *On the Beach* (1959) and *The Guns of Navarone* (1961). He reached the height of his powers with his quiet triumph as Atticus Finch in *To Kill A Mockingbird* (1962). His Best Actor Oscar was the second Academy Award for a Barter alumnus.

*MARGARET WYCHERLY was actually already an established star when she appeared with Barter in the early '40s. An older character actress, her versatility added a considerable dimension to the basically younger Barter company. Her many screen appearances ranged from a refined English lady in *the Thirteenth Chair* (1929) to Gary Cooper's mother in *Sergeant York* (1941), which also featured Bob Porterfield. She remained active in films until her death in 1956, appearing in *Random Harvest* (1942), *Keeper of the Flame* (1942), *The Yearling* (1946), as Jimmy Cagney's notorius mother ("Top of the world, Ma!") in *White Heat* (1949) and in Olivier's *Richard III* (1956). On Broadway, Wycherly gave notable performances in Elmer Rice's *The Adding Machine* (1923), Pirandello's *Six Characters in Search of an Author,* and *Tobacco Road.* Her television credits include *Philco Playhouse, Kraft Theatre, Studio One* and *G.E. Theatre.* Her only venture into series television was, of course, a character part—Mrs. Brown, the possessive mother in the ill-fated 1952 dramatic program, *Claudia, the Story of a Marriage.*

*MARGARET PHILLIPS started at Barter in 1939 before making her Broadway debut in *Proof Through the Night* (1942). She also appeared on the Great White Way in *The Late George Apley* (1944), *Summer and Smoke* (1949) and *The Cocktail Party* (1952). Perhaps her best remembered role was in the powerful 1946 production of *Another Part of the Forest*, which was personally staged by Lillian Hellman. Almost two powerful for the gleeful post-war mood, Hellman's uncompromising drama ran for only 182 performances. Still, Phillips' characterization of Birdie was applauded by the critics. An interesting footnote to the production is that Phillips co-starred with Patricia Neal, who was also at Barter in 1942, and Mildred Dunnock, with whom Bob appeared on Broadway in the '30s. She also appeared in the films, *A Life of Her Own* (1950) and *The Nun's Story* (1959).

*PATRICIA NEAL, as Bob later told it, came to Barter as an apprentice in 1938 telling him she was 18. He found out later she was only 16. The Knoxville native was a member of the company until the war closed Barter's doors and, afterwards, she became a star in Hollywood and on Broadway. Before her much-publicized and tragic stroke, she appeared in *The Fountainhead* (1949), *The Day the Earth Stood Still* (1951) and *Hud* (1963)—an Oscar-winning performance. After her heroic battle to regain speech and movement, she stunned the film world by returning with a superlative characterization in *The Subject Was Roses* (1968). Neal also went on to star in Earl Hamner's popular Christmas special, *The Homecoming*, which became the pilot for *The Waltons* television series. Her own inspiring story has been the subject of a book by Barry Farrell, *Pat and Roald* (Dahl, her writer husband) and a TV movie based on the book starring Glenda Jackson. Her daughter, Teresa, was a Barter apprentice in 1973.

*LARRY GATES was one of several young actors who formed the nucleus of the post-war Barter company. At one point, Gates, Ernest Borgnine, Herb Nelson, Woody Romoff, Elizabeth Wilson and Diane Cilento were all on the payroll together. Originally selected for the Barter by first Award winner Laurette Taylor in 1939, Gates frequently returned to Abingdon, although in demand on Broadway and television.

Patricia Neal returns home to Barter and chats with Rex Partington some 30 years after her stay in Abingdon.
(Photo courtesy of the Barter Theatre)

*ERNEST BORGNINE briefly interrupted his four-and-a-half year stay at Barter to appear on Broadway in *Harvey*. He could have stayed, but he felt he owed Bob Porterfield a debt of gratitude. Borgnine also traveled to Europe with the Barter production of *Hamlet* that played at Denmark's Elsinore Castle (see Chapter Seven). His first big film break came when he played Fatso Judson in *From Here To Eternity* (1953). Other notable film credits include *Vera Cruze* (1954), *Bad Day at Black Rock* (1954), *Marty* (1955), *The Best Things in Life Are Free* (1956), *The Vikings* (1958), *Barabbas* (1962), *The Dirty Dozen* (1967), *Ice Station Zebra* (1968), *The Wild Bunch* (1969), *Willard* (1971), *The Poseidon Adventure* (1972) and *The Emperor of the North Pole* (1973). For four seasons he was at the helm of the P.T. 73 as Commander Quinton McHale in the enormously successful ABC comedy, *McHale's Navy*. When Borgnine was the subject of a '56 episode of *This Is Your Life*, Porterfield was one of the very special guests. The program announced The Ernest Borgnine Trophy—or "Ernie" Award—which would be presented to the Barter actor judged to have given the best performance of the season. The award never really caught on, and presentations stopped after a few years. Borgnine did, however, like so many Barter graduates, stay in touch with Barter's founder until Bob's death.

*ELIZABETH WILSON started with Barter in '42, returning to the company in the late '40s and early '50s. She has achieved her greatest successes on the Broadway stage where she has appeared in *Sticks and Bones* and *Mornings at Seven*, which brought her a Drama Desk Award and the Outer Circle Critics' Award. In addition to her stage work Wilson has appeared in films—*Picnic* (1955), *The Goddess* (1958), Alfred Hitchcock's *The Birds* (1963), *The Graduate* (1967), *The Day of the Dolphin* (1973), *The Prisoner of Second Avenue* (1975), *9 to 5* (1980) and *The Incredible Shrinking Woman* (1980)—and on television, co-starring with George C. Scott in the highly realistic '63 series, *East Side/West Side*, and as Bernard Hughes' wife in *Doc*. She came back to Barter in 1959 to star in *Auntie Mame* and *Bell, Book and Candle*, and in '64 for *Oh Dad, Poor Dad, Mama's Hung You in the Closet and I'm Feelin' So Sad*.

*WOODY ROMOFF, in the Barter company from 1946 to '52, made his New York debut as Gadshill in *Henry IV, Part I*. He soon established himself in New York with such shows as *She Loves Me* and *Cafe Crown*, also appearing in television dramas on *Studio One*, *Omnibus* and *Kraft Television Theatre*. Romoff made a special return visit to Barter during the '70s to star in *Dracula*.

*CLAUDE AKINS appeared with the Barter touring company in 1950, garnering early experience in such plays as *The Heiress* and *Comedy of Errors*. Also featured in that production of *The Heiress* were Elizabeth Wilson and current Barter producing director Rex Partington. Three years later Akins appeared with another Barterite, Ernie Borgnine, in *From Here to Eternity*. His other film credits include *The Caine Mutiny* (1954), Rev. Brown in *Inherit the Wind* (1959) and *Comanche Station* (1960). Akins was active throughout the '50s and '60s on television, appearing in memorable episodes of *The Loretta Young*

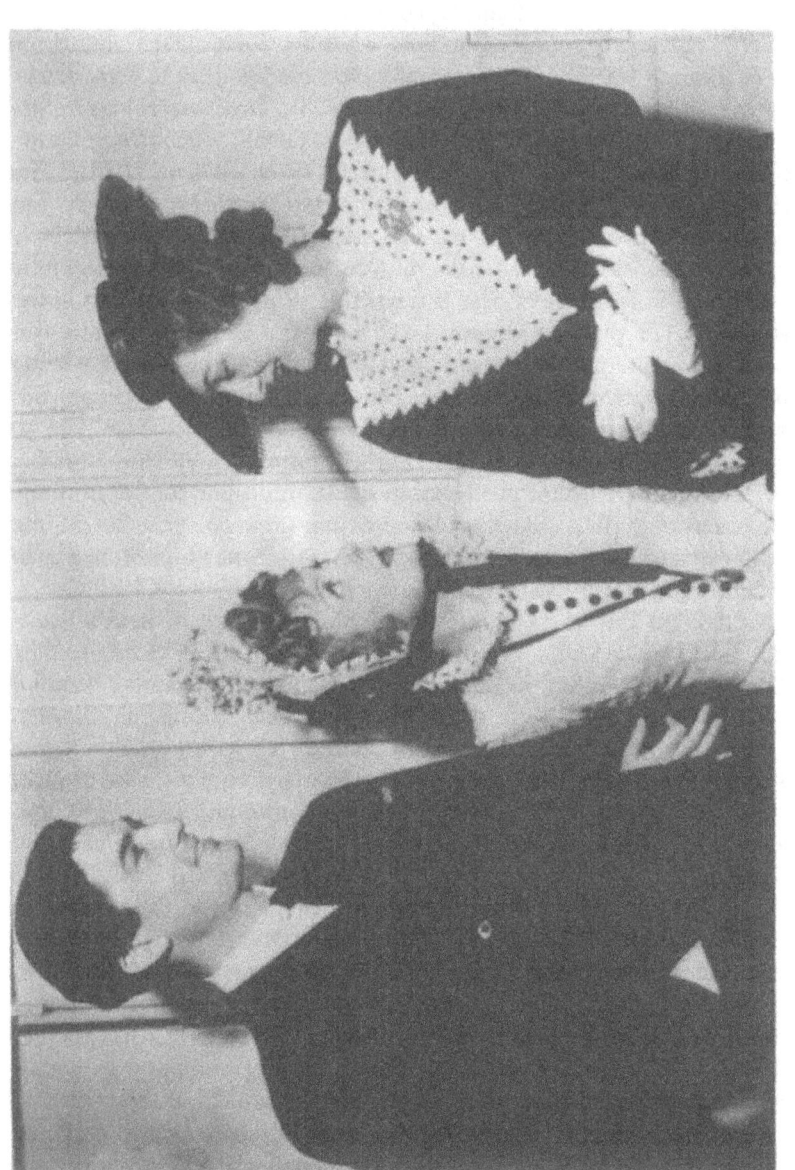

Dorothy Stickney poses between the two promising newcomers she selected to join the Barter company in 1940, Gregoy Peck and Evelyn Wells Fargo. (Photo courtesy of the Barter Theatre)

Show, Bonanza and The Twilight Zone. His greatest notoriety has been from such television series as Movin' On, Nashville 99 and Sheriff Lobo. Long a movie and TV "heavy," he is now one of the most recognized and loved performers on the tube.

*FRITZ WEAVER has enjoyed a long, rewarding career in theater, films and television. He was chosen for the Barter company in 1952 after placing second to Al (David) Hedison in Barter Award auditions conducted by Frederic March and Porterfield. It was so close that they called Hedison and Weaver back for a run-off audition. Weaver left the theater despondent, but Porterfield ran after him and asked him to join the company. Since Hedison was a leading man and Weaver a character actor, it worked out fine. A Barter press release described the actor this way: "Weaver boasts as basic equipment; a natural ease on stage, artistocratic good looks, and a resonant baritone which he attributes to a family line that boasts a number of successful opera singers." He won a Tony Award for Child's Play in the late '60s and played Sherlock Holmes on Broadway in Baker Street. His film credits include Fail-Safe (1964), A Walk in the Spring Rain (1970) and Creepshow (1982), while his television work numbers appearances on Studio One, U.S. Steel Hour, The Twilight Zone, The Fugitive and N.Y.P.D.

*AL (DAVID) HEDISON was chosen for Barter because of his potential as a leading man. After a brief movie career—which included the minor science fiction classic The Fly (1958)—he starred for four seasons as Captain Lee Crane in the popular sci-fi adventure series, Voyage to the Bottom of the Sea. Still a familiar face on network television, Hedison also was the star of Five Fingers, a spy drama that lasted only one season. Trivia buffs can tell you Hedison played Victor Sebastian, an American counterspy whose code name was "five fingers."

*ROSEMARY MURPHY, the other young performer chosen by March for the Barter company, made her Broadway debut in Look Homeward Angel. Her other stage credits include the 1960 production of Period of Adjustment, for which she won an Outer Circle Critics' Award, and Any Wednesday. She also appeared as high school principal Margaret Blumenthal in the 1974 Lucas Tanner TV series, and in the films Berlin Express (1948), The Young Doctors (1961), To Kill A Mockingbird, Any Wednesday (1966), Ben (1972), Walking Tall (1973) and Forty Carats (1973). An insightful observer of the American theater, Murphy contributed several experiences and views to Stuart W. Little and Arthur Cantor's excellent study of Broadway, The Playmakers.

*GRANT WILLIAMS won a spot at Barter in 1953. The actor gained his greatest notoriety in the highly regarded science fiction film, The Incredible Shrinking Man (1957). (Barter coincidences are legion in show business and two Barterites, Ned Beatty and Elizabeth Wilson, ended up in Lily Tomlin's parody, The Incredible Shrinking Woman some 20 years later.) His other film credits include Written on the Wind (1956), Showdown at Abilene (1956), Monolith Monsters (1957) and The Leech Woman (1960). He was also a regular on the Hawaiian Eye television series.

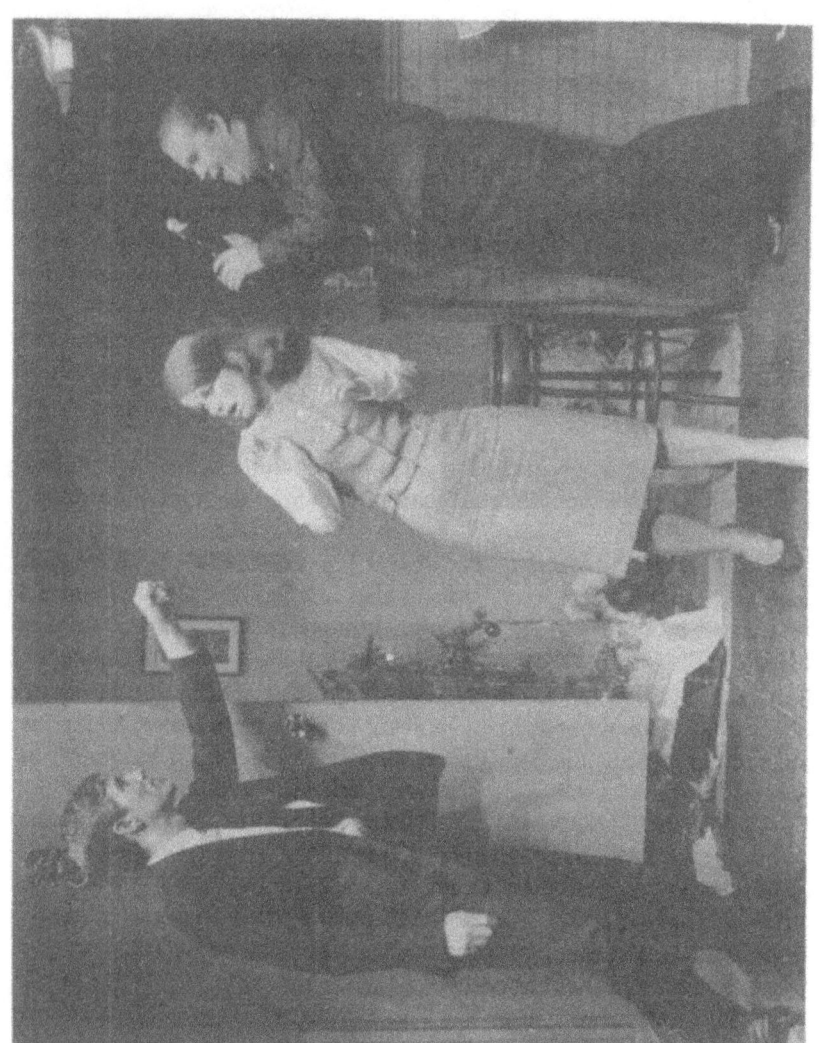

Gary Collins, Flora Elkins and Ned Beatty star in Barter 1963 production of **Period of Adjustment.**
(Photo courtesy of the Barter Theatre)

The Stars of Barter

* HERBERT NELSON returned to Barter over a span of some 20 years. He went on to Broadway, but found steady work in television. He was a regular on *The Brighter Day* and *The Guiding Light* soap operas, and his many television credits include appearances on *Studio One* and *The Ed Sullivan Show*.

* DIANE CILENTO started as an apprentice at Barter for the 1949-50 season. The Australian-born actress made her Broadway debut playing Helen of Troy in *Tiger at the Gates*. Her film work includes *The Breaking Point* (1950), *Wings of Danger* (1952), *The Admirable Crichton* (1957), *The Naked Edge* (1961), *Rattle of a Simple Man* (1964), *The Agony and the Ecstasy* (1965), *Hombre* (1967), *The Wicker Man* (1973), *Hitler: The Last Ten Days* (1974), and her delightful contribution to *Tom Jones* (1963), for which she received an Oscar nomination for Best Supporting Actress.

* NED BEATTY started with Barter as an apprentice in 1958, staying through '64 and appearing as Big Daddy in *Cat On a Hot Tin Roof*, the title role in *Uncle Vanya* and the boy's father in *The Fantasticks*. After a brief return in '67 and a stint at Washington's Arena Stage, Beatty launched a highly successful film career highlighted by his work in *Deliverance* (1972), *Nashville* (1975), an Oscar nomination for *Network* (1976), *Superman* (1978), *1941* (1979) and *Hopscotch* (1981). He has also appeared in a series of well-recieved TV movies that include *Our Town*, *Guyana Tragedy*, *Friendly Fire* and *All the Way Home*.

* ROBERT PASTENE, first at Barter in 1946, became yet another Barter graduate to cut out a successful career in several mediums. His many Broadway shows number *The First Cracus*, *St. Joan*, Maurice Evans' *Hamlet*, *The Children's Hour* and *Taming of the Shrew*. He had a long run on the soap opera, *The Edge of Night*, and for one season he was *Buck Rogers* (1950-51) on the ABC series. His film credits include *Butterfield 8* (1960).

* GEROME RAGNI was chosen for a 1962 trip to Abingdon by Barter Award winner Abe Burrows. During his stay, he appeared with Beatty in the Barter production of *The Fantasticks*. He would go on to write the trend-setting Broadway play of the '60s, *Hair*.

* MITCH (MITCHELL) RYAN was another award winner, picked for the company by no less than Ethel Merman in 1957. He stayed until 1960, returning for the 1963-64 season. His Barter roles include Brick in *Cat on a Hot Tin Roof*, the lead in *Bus Stop*, and John the Witch Boy in *Dark of the Moon*. The ruggedly handsome actor, who appeared on Broadway in *Wait Until Dark*, Brecht's *Baal*, *Othello* (as Iago opposite James Earl Jones), *Moon for the Misbegotten*, the revival of Arthur Miller's *The Price*, and *Medea*, also tried out three short-lived ABC series: *Chase* (1973-74), *Executive Suite* (1976-77), and *Having Babies* (1978). He fared better as Slim in Robert Blake's much-praised TV-movie version of John Steinbeck's *Of Mice and Men*. He played Ernest Hemmingway in the PBS special, *The Hemingway Story*, and his feature films include *Monte Walsh* (1970), *The Hunting Party* (1971), *Electra Glide in Blue* (1973), *The Friends of Eddie Coyle* (1973) and *Magnum Force* (1973). Ryan made one very big hit during his stay in Abingdon, but not on the Barter stage.

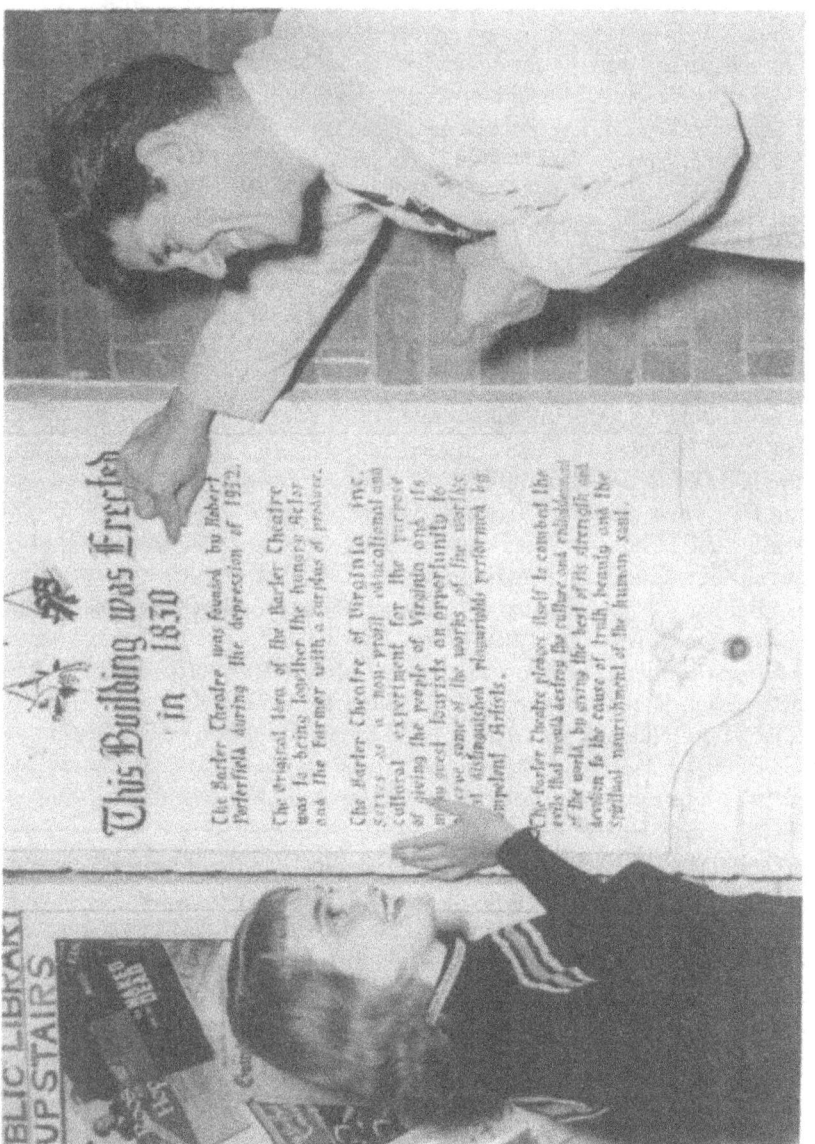

Mr. P shows aspiring actress Diane Cilento the plaque in front of the Barter Theatre.
(Photo courtesy of the Barter Theatre)

During a 1982 visit, Mitchell Ryan shows wife Lynn around the theater where he often starred 20 years earlier.
(Photo courtesy of the Barter Theatre)

He was charged by local police with whistling at a girl from the passenger seat of a car. The incident soon blew over (no pun intended), but Ryan remembers it clearly: "The actual charge was interfering with a female. The judge thought the whole thing was very silly. And the next day the headlines read, 'Mitch Ryan found innocent of interfering with a female'."

*JERRY ODDO also cut out a successful television career, appearing on such shows as *Wagon Train*, *Perry Mason* and *The Untouchables*. An accomplished playwright, several of his works were premiered at the Barter.

The 1940 Barter production of **Lee of Virginia**.
The heavily made-up actor at far right? Gregory Peck.
(Photo courtesy of the Barter Theatre)

*GARY COLLINS was at Barter in '63 and soon after landed the first of four short-lived series: *The Wackiest Ship in the Army* in 1965. This was followed by *The Iron Horse* in '66, *The Sixth Sense* in '72, and *Born Free* in '74. Collins was also featured in ABC's adaptation of Alex Haley's *Roots*, and was announced as the new master of ceremonies for the Miss America pageant in 1982.

*LARRY LINVILLE, Barter class of '64, became nationally known as weak-willed Major Frank Burns on *M*A*S*H* for several seasons.

*DAVID BIRNEY arrived at Barter in '65. He later starred with his wife, Meredith Baxter-Birney, in *Bridget Loves Bernie* (CBS, 1972), and NBC's *Serpico*. Other credits include the film, *Trial By Combat* (1976) and John Carpenter's excellent TV movie, *Someone is Watching Me!* (1978).

*DAVID SELBY was both a director and actor at Barter in 1966. He started out as an apprentice and went on to appear in *Twelfth Night* ("I carried a spear"), *The Crucible, You Never Can Tell, Marat/Sade*, and as Tony Kirby in *You Can't Take It With You*. He also directed one-acts, children's plays and performed Samuel Beckett's one-man, one-act, *Krapp's Last Tape*. Almost immediately after leaving Barter, the actor landed a role in ABC's immensely successful supernatural soap opera, *Dark Shadows*. Cast as the silent ghost of Quentin Collins, Selby soon found himself featured in teen and horror magazines alike. He has been seen on Broadway in *Sticks and Bones* with Elizabeth Wilson and *Hedda Gabler* with Jane Alexander, while his movie credits include *Night of Dark Shadows* (1971), *Up the Sandbox* (1972) with Barbara Streisand, *The*

When Ralph Edwards devoted a segment of **This Is Your Life** *to Ernest Borgnine, one of the featured guests was Robert Porterfield.*
(Photo courtesy of the Barter Theatre)

Years after his stint at Barter, Gregory Peck is visited in his Hollywood dressing room by Robert Porterfield. (Photo courtesy of the Barter Theatre)

Supercops (1974) with Ron Liebman, *Raise the Titanic* (1980) and *Rich and Famous* (1981) with Jacqueline Bisset and Candice Bergen. Selby is again a familiar face on television due to his portrayal of the daring and smooth-talking Michael Tyrone on NBC's *Flamingo Road*.

*RICHARD SANDERS played a variety of roles in 1972 for Barter's new producing director, Rex Partington. Since 1978 he has been featured as wimpy newsman Les Nessman on the CBS-TV series, *WKRP in Cincinnati*.

And that's just 28 of Barter's more conspicuous graduates. If Barter were a high-visibility theater located in a major metropolitan area, such an honor roll, while still impressive, would be somewhat more understandable. Instead, the Barter is a company where most actors are getting their first or near first taste of theater. How then did this quaint little theater born in the Depression again and again produce performers of such stature? One reason is quickly supplied by Fritz Weaver:

"There is no training like that theater—the trouping, the extension of your own resources. Gregory Peck once told me that everything he learned about acting he got at the Barter."

Claude Akins agreed with that assessment. "It was my first real theater job and I was actually getting paid for it," he recalled. "I remember traveling from town to town, setting up scenery and lights on those gruelling tours. There's no experience like that."

And Ned Beatty nearly echoed the sentiments of his fellow actors during a 1981 visit: "I can't say enough about this place. I almost became a minister and that stage turned out to be my seminary. Literally, there is nothing better for a young actor to do than be in a company like this. Nothing even close."

"It was through Barter that I became an actress," Elizabeth Wilson said in a 1963 interview, "and probably (I) would not have tried to make a career if I had not been in Abingdon."

Barter not only offered a young actor the romance of an extremely colorful theater but also an opportunity to prove himself under the most testing conditions. Under such a challenging set-up, the good and the very good tend to rise to the top. No one was tested harsher than Gregory Peck. On his arrival in Abingdon, he was given 102 pages to memorize in one day for a role in *Button, Button*. He also drove the truck and set up scenery while trying to master the dialogue. The young actor had to ad-lib some of the dialogue, but he got through it. Winning the Oscar was probably a cinch next to that little miracle.

But, clearly, another primary reason for Barter's proficiency in the star department was Robert Porterfield's distinct ability to recognize talent. No one would dare claim that Mr. P. was the greatest actor or director to hit the American stage. And, it is generally conceded that his greatest gift was promotion. True enough, through his undeniable charm and genius for publicity, Porterfield promoted his theater to an international reputation. Still, too often overlooked was his knack for spotting and nurturing raw acting ability.

"Bob could spot talent," Weaver pointed out. "He could see it under layers

During the Abingdon run of **Family Portrait**, *legendary actress Judith Anderson sits at the dressing table salvaged from New York's Empire Theatre.*
(Photo courtesy of the Barter Theatre)

Judith Anderson poses with the cast of **Family Portrait**.
(Photo courtesy of the Barter Theatre)

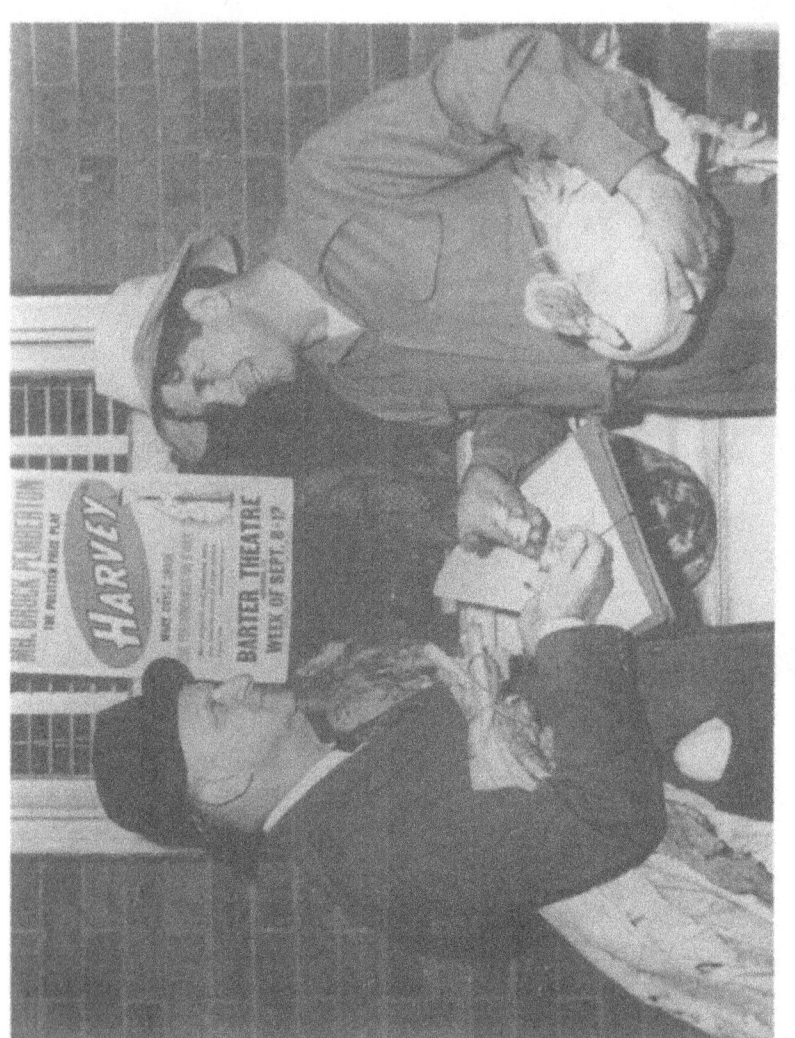

Broadway producer Brock Pemberton accepts his pay in "barter" from Bob Porterfield when starring in the theater's production of **Harvey**.
(Photo courtesy of the Barter Theatre)

and layers of camouflage and go after it. Like with Gregory Peck, Bob forced him to tell him stories to draw him out. With me, he once told me casually, 'You're a very passionate man. I'd like to see more of that on stage.' Well, I had been talking about something in a very animated way, but I had never thought of myself that way. It was like a door opening. He knew it was there."

"He was always like a father-figure to me," Beatty commented. "He had a way of encouraging you and keeping you going. He truly liked actors."

And, these "stars" all have their favorite Barter memories and warm tributes to Bob Porterfield.

When Barter's founder died in 1971, Gregory Peck admitted that "if it were not for Robert Porterfield, I doubt very seriously if I would have even had an acting career."

Some years later, he remembered when theatergoers actually brought vegetables, hams, livestock and crafts to "barter" for admission—"I am here as one who ate the box office...he (Porterfield) was a warm, wonderful man. When I complained once about having to memorize 110 pages of dialogue in three days, Bob told me perhaps the best advice I've ever had: If you have to do it, grit your teeth, hold on and go with it."

"Bob knew what he was doing...it was a real baptism by fire...it was a close friendship. Bob told me to always serve it up with a little gravy when you want to entertain people. I remember this tonight with some feeling of discomfort because even today I am not the storyteller that Bob Porterfield was."

"He was the courtliest of men," Weaver reminisced. "He had that smile that was just out of this world. He just laughed you out of any temper. He was a natural kind of con man, but in the best way. He always told you he was doing it. If he said, 'Go in the street and let yourself get run over,' we would have done it."

David Selby is an excellent example of how Barter gave young actor's the opportunity to grow rapidly: "Growing up in West Virginia, I only thought of theater. I had done some theater as a kid, but just getting out of West Virginia was a little difficult. Barter was my first real job in theater and I want to tell you, I worked like the devil. Peter Culman was actually running things that year and I started out as an apprentice. I started building sets and carrying spears. Then I went from an Equity journeyman to a full member company to some lead roles and some directing. I ran the gamut and had a marvelous time."

"I lived at the Barter Inn and by the time I left I was making Equity scale, which was about $70 or $80 a week. Of course, Barter also provided room and board. We were so busy, but I wouldn't change a thing, you can't replace those times."

Selby also has some special memories of Bob Porterfield and Abingdon.

"I remember each year they used to give away an acre of land to the Barter Award winner. We used to tease Bob and say, 'What are you going to do if all those people come and claim their acres of land.' "

"One special memory I have of Barter is the night two kittens were left in a

Delightful old character actor Eric Blore mugs for a shot in the Barter offices.
(Photo courtesy of the Barter Theatre)

box outside the stage door. My wife and another actor each took one and when I got home from the play, there was this little calico kitten waiting for me. Well, I didn't want to keep it, but the more I started playing with it, the more I grew to like it. That cat has gone everywhere with us. I still have it."

"All my feelings about Barter are very special."

And, no matter how many credits they amass, each Barter "star" remembers Abingdon with a nostalgic smile.

"I can't tell you what memories this brings back," Mitch Ryan said while standing stage-center during a visit some 20 years after his Barter stint. "Bob used to stand all the way in the back during rehearsals and yell, 'I can't hear you, honey!' It's one of the greatest theaters in the world for training. Rosemary Murphy told me the same thing. If you've got any talent at all, you get great parts here and the chance to chew them up."

"I got here in 1957 and was paid the handsome salary of $50 a week. My first show at Barter was *Bus Stop*. My favorite show was *Cat On a Hot Tin Roof*. I played Brick and Ned Beatty was Big Daddy. I liked that show because Bob was scared of it. He thought it was too rough for this area. I saw Bob in New York and California from time to time. We'd have lunch at the Algonquin—that's where he stayed when he'd come to New York for a visit. I couldn't get to the memorial service they had at Sardi's. Elizabeth Wilson called me in 1971 to tell me they were having it. You know, after I went to Hollywood, I became Mitchell Ryan. Bob never liked that. He always preferred Mitch Ryan."

Acting hasn't been the only realm of theater to which Barter has made contributions. Three playwrights—William Gibson (*Two for the Seesaw* and *The Miracle Worker*), Edith Sommers (*A Roomful of Roses*), and Sam Taylor (*Sabrina Fair* and *The Pleasure of His Company*)—spent the summer of 1939 in Abingdon. Bob had a great respect for writers and often thought of starting an actual artists' colony in Abingdon, setting aside some land for small lodgings where playwrights, poets, artists and directors could spend a summer in blissful creation.

And, occasionally, an established performer or playwright would use Abingdon as a showcase for their abilities. Mary Chase (*Harvey*), another close friend of Bob's, chose Barter to premiere her *Mr. Thing* in 1951 (later reworked as *Mrs. McThing* for a Broadway production with Helen Hayes and Barter graduate Ann Buckles). Tennessee Williams came to Abingdon in 1963 to oversee the premiere of his revised *The Milktrain Doesn't Stop Here Anymore*.

Colorful Broadway producer Brock Pemberton got a taste of the other side of his business when he starred at Barter as Elwood P. Dowd in *Harvey*. The legendary Judith Anderson agreed to star in *Family Portrait* in the mid-'50s and, over 25 years later, Dame Judith found herself touring in *Medea* with Zoe Caldwell and two former Barterites—Rosemary Murphy and Mitchell Ryan. Dennis King headed the 1959 cast of *Separate Tables*, while delightful old character actor Eric Blore found his way to Barter, as did Guy Kibbee.

But, for the most part, the accent at Barter has been on the promising new performer.

"I think the people of Abingdon thought of us as Bob's big expensive hobby," Weaver said. "Mostly I remember hushed streets and audiences that took us to their hearts. I also remember I fell in love regularly at Barter."

Akins got his first big break indirectly through Porterfield. Just a couple years after his Barter stint, the young actor was interviewing with a New York casting director. To his surprise, the agent asked about Bob Porterfield when he saw the Barter credit, and Akins ended up in *From Here to Eternity*.

Beatty remembered that it was on the opening night of Bernard Shaw's *Misalliance* when his first wife gave birth to fraternal twins. During the run of another play, Beatty's wife was taken to the hospital maternity room in between a matinee and evening performance.

"A typical actor, I was only thinking of myself," he related with a grin. "As she was being wheeled off to the maternity room, I yelled, 'Wish me luck, honey!' These are true stories. They have to be."

He also recalled touring in Southwest Virginia where, due to his long hair and bulk, little kids would ask if he was a wrestler. He always pretended he was.

Before Beatty could move on to another story, he was rudely interrupted by the fire siren on Barter's roof. It's always been there, and the standing rule is that the actors freeze if the whistle sounds during a performance. Hardly annoyed by the shrillness, the genial character actor clapped his hands together and exclaimed, "I love it!"

"One of my warmest memories is Bob Porterfield's curtain speech," he said. "He knew where his laughs were. I can still remember punching him through the curtain saying, 'get off, get off.' I never wanted the season to end."

Chapter Seven: Changes At Barter

For fifty years—forty with Porterfield and ten under Rex Partington—Barter has been a theater that has stressed both tradition and innovation. Like the town it calls home, Barter holds on to those traditions and ideals that audiences new and old find so delightful. It's a theater with a lot of heritage and neither Porterfield nor Partington has ever tried to deny those things that make Barter so unique.

That can be a hinderance, of course, especially when local audiences react negatively to new and challenging elements in "their" Barter Theatre. The resistance Bob met, for instance, when he instituted a cash box office was typical. Local audiences didn't stop to think that this change meant better, more professional productions. It meant they could no longer bring carrots in exchange for a ticket. The economic realities of theater did not concern them. All they knew was they wanted their Barter like it used to be.

Fortunately, Porterfield was a diplomat par excellent, while Partington has been able to walk that tricky line of progress and preservation.

The city jail may no longer be underneath the stage, but the fire whistle still sits on the Barter roof. Most patrons buy their tickets with cash, but the market equivalent in "barter" will still get you through the door. It's change and tradition, holdovers and innovations existing side by side in a theater rich with history.

One can still find in the basement of the Barter Inn a rickety sign removed from a dilapidated old pick-up that reads: "Gregory Peck drove this truck."

That's a reminder of Barter's past, but also a suggestion that the actors we now see at Barter are the future Gregory Pecks and Patricia Neals.

That spirit and sentiment is evident before every performance when Partington closes his front-of-curtain speech with Bob Porterfield's now famous adage: "If ya' like us, talk about us. If ya' don't, jes keep ya mouth shut!"

Still, Porterfield and Partington both believed that vital theater meant progress. So, rather than settle into your average summer stock theater or some kind of quaint tourist attraction, Barter has seen its share of change since 1946.

Until Robert Porterfield's death in 1971, the biggest change was state funding and, ultimately, a switch to Equity contracts. There were, of course, a lot of little heartbreaks and victories along the way.

July 10, 1947 looms grimly among the disappointments. It was the first time in Barter's history that a performance had to be cancelled. They had been scheduled to perform *East Lynne* at the Dobyns-Bennett High School auditorium in Kingsport when a fire swept through the nearly deserted facility.

Howard Lindsay and wife Dorothy Stickney ham it up during a trip to Abingdon that coincided with a production of **Arsenic and Old Lace**.
(Photo courtesy of the Barter Theatre)

Luckily, most of the company was at dinner. It took volunteer firemen over an hour to bring the blaze under control, but costumes, sets, props and equipment valued at between $2,500 and $3,000 were lost.

Porterfield had stepped up Barter's touring after the war, frequently offering three different companies during winter months. Barter moved well beyond the limits of Southwest Virginia and Upper East Tennessee, and wherever they went—major cities or the West Coast—reaction was favorable.

"The first result at seeing the play (*Much Ado About Nothing*) at George Washington High School in Alexandria is to suggest that what this country needs is 47 other state theaters," wrote *Washington Evening Star* critic Jay Carmody in 1946. "The second and correlative thought of the spectator is that the Virginia Conservation Commission never spent a wiser $10,000."

Of all the Barter tours, none received more ballyhoo than *The Virginian* in the early '50s. It was staged by Margaret Perry and starred Porterfield in the title role. Also on that tour were Cleo Holladay, Frank Lowe, Bob Gallico and Owen Phillips, all of whom immediately smile when the production is mentioned.

An informal backstage shot of Bob Porterfield during the early '50s tour of **The Virginian**. *They were touring Owen Wister's classic western, but the folks flocked to see Bob in the title role.*
(Photo courtesy of the Barter Theatre)

"They came to see Bob Porterfield," Gallico commented, "and that's really what he gave them. It wasn't until *The Virginian* tour that we really got close; sitting up nights talking on the bus."

Lowe uses practically the same words: "Traveling with him on *The Virginian* tour was when I really got to know him."

"He had a great time with that part," Holladay recalled. "Of course, he got by a lot on his charm. Owen was Owen Wister (the author of *The Virginian*) and Bob was the Virginian. But he was Bob. He didn't overcome his personality in that part. But he did use it."

Robert Porterfield administers western justice in this scene from
The Virginian.
(Photo courtesy of the Barter Theatre)

What could have been a major triumph for Barter turned into an experience no one much likes to discuss in detail—The Elsinore *Hamlet*. Since 1937, the Danish National Theatre has invited national theaters from other countries to perform William Shakespeare's *Hamlet* in the courtyard of Kronborg Castle. America did not have a national company, however. But Virginia did have a State Theatre. So, in 1947, Porterfield received an invitation for Barter to stage *Hamlet* at the 1949 two-week Hamlet Festival.

The Barter company performing **Hamlet** *at Kronborg Castle in Denmark.*
(Photo courtesy of the Barter Theatre)

The problem was money. Barter could hardly subsidize the trip from its own coffers, not even with the state funding. Yet, the prestige attached to such an undertaking was just too tempting to pass up. Once again Bob turned to a New York friend for help.

In this case, it was Robert Breen, an actor he'd met while in Texas during his hitch with the Air Force. Breen had been fascinated by Porterfield's plans for a national theater, and from their brainstorming came the realization of the American National Theatre and Academy (ANTA) in 1945. It all stemmed from Bob's rather utopian plans for elevating theaters on a national basis through state companies. ANTA had even been chartered by Congress before the war, but federal funds were never realized. After the war, largely inspired by Porterfield, the tireless Breen slaved to make ANTA a viable force.

Breen, executive secretary of ANTA in 1947, asked the State Department to co-sponsor the trip with his organization. In the meantime, although financial backing was hardly secured, Breen told his friend to accept the invitation. He also offered to direct and star in the production for Bob.

It was already slipping away from being an actual Barter production when Blevins Davis, an extremely affluent ANTA board member, put up the necessary funds. There were stipulations which Porterfield was in no position to debate. Davis wanted to be able to select the show's designers.

Plans went ahead and *Hamlet* became Barter's 200th production, staged in Abingdon as the last show of the 1948 season.

In one sense, Bob got what he wanted. The Elsinore Trip generated a great deal of publicity in the American and Danish press. After all, Olivier and Gielgud had performed the role in Demark, and now the Americans would show what they could do. *Time* magazine described Barter as "far and away the most active professional repertory company touring the U.S." The story also noted that the Elsinore "Barter" company would be "bolstered" by such Broadway veterans as Breen, Aline MacMahon as the Queen, Walter Abel as the King, and Clarence Derwent as Polonius.

Clearly, the production had ceased to be a genuine Barter offering. Several company members resented having to "make way" for imported talent after creating these roles in Abingdon, but they had no choice. The generosity of others came with strings attached. Among the Barter regulars who did make the trip was Ernest Borgnine.

Reviews of *Hamlet* were largely negative. And three of the performers criticized were Breen, Abel and MacMahon. Richard L. Coe of the *Washington Post*, a Barter booster for several years, also found little good to say about the stars in the Elsinore production. Coe said he liked Derwent's Polonius, and noted the overall reaction from Danish audiences had "hardly been lavish in praise."

One telling sign appeared when the company moved on to Germany. There the production was billed as "Blevins Davis presents Hamlet." Even the brilliant critic Brooks Atkinson failed to mention Barter in his incisive *Broadway*. Although he describes ANTA at length and lists the Elsinore *Hamlet* among its accomplishments, there is not a word about Barter or Bob Porterfield.

Barter still holds the distinction of being the only American theater invited to stage *Hamlet* at Elsinore. The honor must be footnoted, however, with the fact that the Danes didn't really see the Barter Theatre in action.

A story which had a much more satisfying ending followed soon after Elsinore. Never were Porterfield's enterprising ways more in evidence than in 1953 when he heard the majestic old Empire Theatre in New York was slated for destruction. Immediately he was on the phone.

"What's going to happen to that marvelous old curtain?" was his feverish question. "And that marvelous carpet? And those marvelous seats? And those marvelous golden lamps outside the front door?"

"Junk," the owner replied to Porterfield's obvious delight. "You want those, Mr. Porterfield?"

The Empire Theatre was New York's oldest legitimate theater, built in 1893 and opulently furnished in red and gold roccoco. There were gilded fixtures, crystal chandeliers, magnificent mirrors, and seats all adorned with a gold needlepoint "E". It had been sold to M. Lowenstein and Sons, Inc. by the Astor family and Bob quickly asked Lady Astor for the interior furnishings. He was told he could have anything he could carry away, but there was one hitch—it was Friday and the theater would be torn down on Monday.

Porterfield and his staff got on the phones to friends and Barter alumni in New York. With vans and trucks supplied by a Virginia firm, company members were dispatched from Abingdon, while Bob coordinated the massive salvage maneuver at home. Working through the weekend, the assemblage removed $75,000 worth of properties and loaded them on vans before the wreckers could move in.

"I knew Bob Porterfield in New York and was invited to several of the Barter Award dinners," actor Harry Ellerbe reminisced. "The old Empire Theatre in New York was an extremely special theater for me. I had done Ibsen's *Ghosts* at the Empire with Alla Nazimova, who I think no actress has ever touched in sheer brilliance. It was a brilliant success.

"Five years later, I was directing a play called *Sailor's Delight* and rehearsing it in the Empire's office. The secretary came in and said, 'Why don't you go down and take a final look? This is the day they're dismantling the inside.' Well, I knew it was slated to be torn down, but I didn't realize it was so soon. It upset me so much and here were these kids tearing everything up.

"One tall, red-haired pimply faced kid shouted at me, 'Hey, you can't go in there. Mr. Porterfield says to keep people out.' Finally, one young actor recognized me and explained that everything in the theater had been given to Bob Porterfield provided he could get them out before it was torn down."

The young man asked Ellerbe if he'd like a souvenir from the Empire—perhaps one of the ornate gold "E's" from the back of a seat. At first, the idea seemed morbid, but since Sardi's and the Players Club had both asked for mementos, he reconsidered and still has the framed seat-covering.

Twenty-three years later, Ellerbe visited Abingdon for his friend Will Geer's one-man benefit for Barter. Producing director Rex Partington asked him to come back for a production and, when he stepped on the stage of the Barter Theatre to play Grandpa in *You Can't Take It With You*, there were the furnishings, lamps, chandeliers, trim and seats he saw being taken from his beloved Empire.

"I was so thrilled and delighted by the whole thing," he said. "There's nothing quite like this theater. It's unique."

Frank Lowe remembers the Empire Theater convoy from another vantage point. He was one of the actors dispatched to New York from Abingdon: "There were about six of us from the theater. We were told to look for everything and we did—seats, drapes, materials, electrical and technical equipment, light fixtures...anything that could be used in Abingdon."

Now the Empire lives on in Abingdon. When the curtain went up on the 1953 season, Barter patrons were dazzled by three ornate chandeliers and several bronze candelabra requiring more than 500 light bulbs, sumptuous red seats emblazoned with the famous golden "E," and a stirring portrait of Katherine Cornell.

Opening night - 1950.
(Photo courtesy of the Barter Theatre)

The '50s saw other changes at Barter. Ever thinking of new things to try, Bob instituted after-theater parties and receptions in 1953. Generally set up at the Martha Washington Inn or across the street at the Cave House, a Main Street craft shop near the theater, these get-togethers were humorously dubbed "Chez Robert" (pronounced Shay Row-bare).

"The townspeople used to call it the Cheese Robert," Mary Dudley said with a laugh.

Of course, a great deal of attention was bestowed on Barter when Borgnine won the Best Actor Oscar for *Marty*. The event prompted the *Bristol Herald-Courier* to write; "Barter has won an inimitable spot in the theatrical world simply by virtue of consistently superlative work....But we also pay our respects to Barter, realizing that its importance lies not in whether its 'alumni' win awards, but in the continuing part which the theater of Abingdon plays in the social, economic, cultural and civic life in our area. Academy Awards will come and go. Barter will remain."

Changes At Barter

*The year was 1954 and the play was **Lolita**, the premiere of Mary Chase's new comedy.*
(Photo courtesy of the Barter Theatre)

A Barter tradition until 1958: Bob welcomes Mary Balance on opening night.
(Photo courtesy of the Barter Theatre)

Anniversaries also came and went. Mary Balance, an elderly Abingdon native who had attended every Barter opening night since 1933, was the guest of honor at the 25th anniversary. Born Dec. 15, 1864, the night Union troops burned the Abingdon courthouse, she was one of Barter's most colorful patrons. Each June, area newspapers were bound to have a picture of Porterfield welcoming Mary Balance to opening night ceremonies. She died at the age of 93 in October, 1958.

Bob remarked on the occasion of the 25th anniversary, "It doesn't seem 25 years since a dollar wasn't anywhere to be seen. Today, they go so fast you don't see them anyway. A lot has happened in 25 years—lots of happy things, and a lot of unhappy things; but, all in all, I've lived and, boy! have I had a good time."

Five years later, President John F. Kennedy sent a note of congratulations for the 30th anniversary: "This unique enterprise shows us all that the best theater, both old and new, finds a lively response among the people and meets a real need of the community....Thirty years is a long time in the life of a man and even in the life of an institution. Yet thirty years of productive existence are now

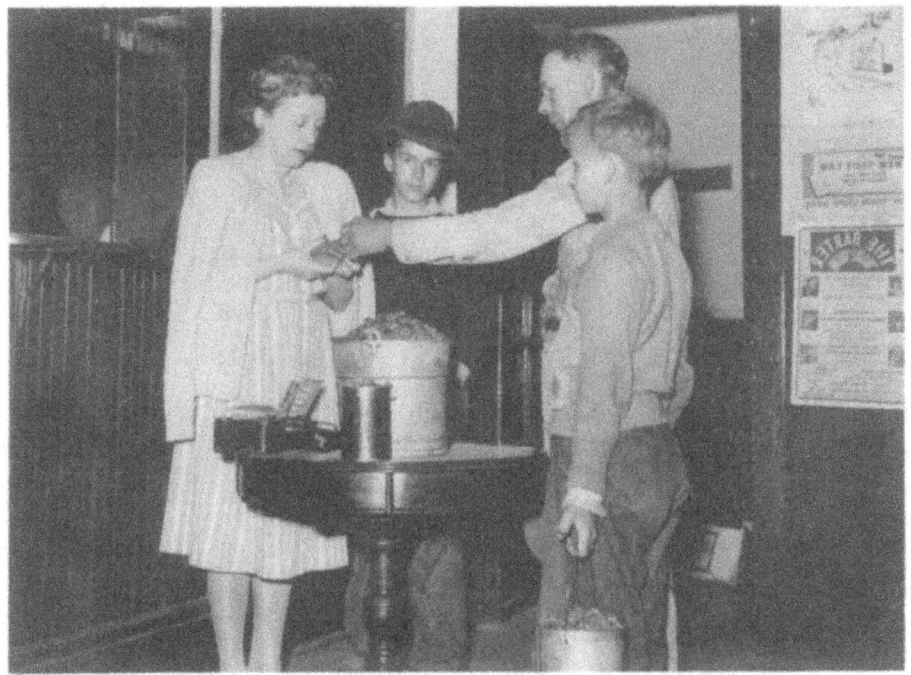

A devoted Barter supporter, Alice Hilton accepts "barter" at the box office during the late '40s.
(Photo courtesy of the Barter Theatre)

marked by the Barter Theatre, and thirty years of effort and success by its founder and guiding spirit, Robert Porterfield. I send my sincere congratulations. I am confident the Barter Theatre in the years ahead will grow even further in stature and influence."

For this anniversary Porterfield quipped, "The past thirty years has been full of the magic of make-believe. That is, making believe the Barter Theatre has all the equipment and money that other professional theaters have."

The year 1962 was tinged with sadness for Barter by the passing of Alice Hilton, a woman whose contributions to the theater can hardly be overstated. Pearl Hayter, who worked closely with Alice for many years and succeeded her as business manager recalls that "while many people have taken and received much from Barter, Alice Hilton gave completely of herself for so many year. She always kept a low profile and she didn't want the recognition, but she was here from the late '40s to 1962 in a volunteer capacity. She was completely devoted to Bob and the Barter. She paid for the air conditioning in the theater and a new marquee. She gave of herself financially and as a volunteer. She believed if you were here for the benefit of the theater, you deserved a place."

The Barter Theatre as it appeared in 1965 welcoming First Lady Lady Bird Johnson.
(Photo courtesy of the Barter Theatre)

Bob Porterfield escorts First Lady Lady Bird Johnson during her 1965 visit to Abingdon.
(Photo courtesy of the Barter Theatre)

Lady Bird Johnson is greeted by a well-wisher while awaiting the curtain to go up on the first act at the Barter Theatre.
(Photo courtesy of the Barter Theatre)

The years were also full of honors and awards. Most prominent was Bob's 1948 Antoinette Perry Award (Tony) for contributions to the American theater. That award was particularly touching for Bob since the later executive director of the American Theatre Wing for whom the award was named was one of Barter's earliest supporters. Bob was also honored with an Honorary Doctor of Literature from Hampden-Sydney College in 1948; named First Citizen of Abingdon by the Town Council in 1957; given the Thomas Jefferson Award for his public relations work on behalf of Virginia in 1963; and presented with the Suzanne David Memorial Award at the 1967 Southeastern Theatre Conference.

Bob and Barter were also featured in an article by Joseph R. Judge, "The Story of Barter Theatre," which was written for the magazine *Amerika* published by the State Department for distribution in Russia. Judge dealt at length with the Empire Theatre adventure, noting the crew "received the thanks of Mr. P. And very often that's its own best reward, for there is a feeling, undiscouraged by Porterfield, that when you do something for Barter you also do something for the whole theater and the national culture as well. It is that kind of feeling that has kept Barter young and growing all these years."

But in spite of the recognition, accomplishments and honors, Bob was worried about Barter's future. He recounted one sobering trip in 1960: "I came through Dallas on the way back and there is the Margo Jones Theater closed. Nobody ever did more for decentralized theater than Margo. But two years after Margo died, the theater folded up. Now I can't let that happen to Barter. I'm not going to live forever, but the Barter should go on. It has become important to the theater world and important to Virginia."

To insure Barter's survival, Bob set up the Barter Theatre Foundation, which still administers the theater's activities through an 11-member Board of Directors.

Bob also set up the Friends of Barter, an organization made up basically of area residents that runs annual season ticket campaigns.

And there was an expansion in actual theater activities. In 1961, Bob opened the Barter Playhouse, located across the street from the theater. The oldest of all the Barter buildings, it was constructed as a Protestant Methodist Church in 1830. Porterfield asked the owners, the Methodist Conference and Emory and Henry College, if he could clean out the structure and use it as a theater. For the most part, the Playhouse was used for children's shows, experimental drama and avant-garde theater.

"He'd let you do just about anything over in the Playhouse," Ned Beatty pointed out. "That's where we did shows that might have been too risque for the usual theater audiences. I remember I talked him into letting us do *Don Juan in Hell* over there. I was really enthusiastic about it and he let us do it—even though nobody really knew the show around here, it was way too difficult for, and realizing how audiences would probably react to four characters sitting on stools for an entire show. But I wanted to do *Don Juan in Hell.*"

Porterfield did try to ease his control of Barter a little after he married Mary Dudley. In 1966, he took a year-long leave-of-absence and toured Europe, leaving 26-year-old Peter Culman in charge.

Culman had been at Barter in 1960 and '61 as a production coordinator, a title he still doesn't understand.

"I asked what's the production coordinator," Culman remembered. "And he said, 'Honey, you make things happen.' "

The army interrupted his Barter career for three years, but he was back for the '65 season as associate director and vice-president of the Barter foundation. Again he was asked to make things happen.

It was Culman's idea to turn the church into the Barter Playhouse.

"Well," Mr. P told him, "You're the twentieth person in twenty years to come up with that idea. If you think you can do it, go ahead."

"I hesitate to say we were close friends personally, but we were close friends professionally," Culman explained. We were totally different in our approaches. He was by the seat of his pants. He relished chances. He almost lived by

The Barter Theatre as it appeared in the mid-60's. The man looking on from the extreme left is Robert Porterfield.
(Photo courtesy of the Barter Theatre)

disorganization. But it worked. The genius of the guy was that he had great horse sense. While I couldn't dispute his success, we were totally different.

"Bob was a gambler. He took a chance on me. He'd let you try something. He'd say, 'Go ahead, honey. See what happens.' When he wanted to take off for a year, I asked if I could take over. There was no magical selection process. It was a delightful year from all viewpoints. From my viewpoint, being 26-years-old and running a theater, it was great.

"It was a terrific interlude for me. But it wasn't always rosey because Bob and I were so different. I stood up to him and he ran all over everybody with his charm. He slaughtered them with it. It was an admirable kind of manipulation. And it worked more often than it didn't."

Bob never threw anything out, a philosophy Culman certainly didn't adhere to.

"My philosophy was, when in doubt, throw it out," Culman said. "His desk was piled high with stacks of paper. He'd say he knew where everything was and I'd say, "bull." We must have made 50 trips to the dump during my stay there, but he never interfered with any decision I'd make. He did used to get mad as hell at me."

When Bob returned to Barter, Culman felt it was time to move on.

"I couldn't go back to being just a member of the company," he commented. "I had outgrown myself at Barter."

Culman went directly from Barter to Center Stage in Baltimore where he continues as managing director. Some felt Bob was grooming Culman as a "potential successor," but Culman is the first to admit that he didn't really fit the spirit of Barter's founder.

Pearl Hayter remembers Culman as a "dedicated and hardworking" young man, "but nobody was ready for anybody to take Porterfield's place."

While many things changed at Barter, Bob's overwhelming personality remained the same. He still called everyone "honey." He still looked for every possible way to promote his theater. And he continued looking around for a possible successor. One man he kept his eye on was Rex Partington.

Owen Phillips as he appeared as Owen Wister in **The Virginian**.
(Photo courtesy of the Barter Theatre)

Chapter Eight: Talking With Owen

He settles down in the sitting room of his quaint Barter Inn apartment after making sure his guest's coffee cup is filled. Before we fall to talking about Barter in earnest, a rather animated dachsund makes his presence known, striving mightily for attention.

He doesn't get too far before his master waves a stern, admonishing finger.

"We're working," says Owen Phillips, and Sam retreats to other, less preoccupied quarters.

Through much of Barter's history, Bob Porterfield's closest friend was his frequent director and sometime actor, Owen Phillips. Eyes sparkling, the wiry, white-haired Owen recalls the man he calls a brother.

"He always had the farm, Twin Oaks," he says, fingertips together, his head at a slight forward incline. "We had an agreement. When he was at the farm, we wouldn't talk about the theater. He was a fine producer and a marvelous public relations man. Because of him, this is one of the very few theaters in the country with a heart. There's something about this place that keeps drawing you back."

Owen should know. He first arrived at Barter in 1935, after heading the drama department at the Cincinnati Conservatory of Music and directing the Cincinnati Actor's Guild. He stayed for two seasons in Abingdon, directing and appearing in shows, and returning in 1946. This time he was with the Barter company for ten years, leaving to direct at Florida's Cocoanut Grove, where he opened two of Tennessee Williams' reworked *The Milktrain Doesn't Stop Here Anymore*, rejoining Barter to stay in 1968.

"I had never heard of Barter Theatre in 1934, but I was intrigued," Owen says in a soft, deliberate voice. "We had our hands full. It was rugged. But right from the start you could tell this theater was built on love. I was immediately glad I made the decision to come here."

Owen is quick to stress that Barter was not started on some harebrained whim:

"Apparently, Bob tested the waters in 1931. He was home for a little while and wanted to try to put together a show. He gave a talk at Emory and Henry College and he made it sound so exciting that everybody wanted to go to New York and be an actor. His idea was something like Bob Porterfield's Theater Guild of Southwest Virginia. They somehow managed a production of *Hay Fever*, but Bob had proved to himself there was an audience for live theater here."

During his many years at Barter, Owen practically did it all—directing, acting, producing, public relations, touring. He also got to see many sides of Bob Porterfield both personally and professionally.

The 1952 production of **The Curious Savage** *with Owen Phillips, Cleo Holladay and Dorothy LaVern.*
(Photo courtesy of the Barter Theatre)

"We were like brothers," he declares. "He was filled with a radiance and personality and terrific love of theater which gave him the drive he needed. Bob was very progressive in his approach to theater. I don't think he did as many new things as Rex tries to do but he loved new things. And Bob loved this area so much. He got a stimulation which came from being with his own."

Journalists, scholars, actors new to Barter, apprentices, directors, faithful patrons, Barter veterans—sooner or later they all are subdued by Owen's softspoken manner, listening intently to the memories and wisdom of over 50 years in the theater. When someone wants to know about Bob and Barter, they invariably end up talking to Owen.

"When Bob directed," he continues, "he picked people who almost fit the parts personally. And he did plays he knew very well. It wasn't his first love. He loved to see other people doing it."

"Bob was something of a glamour boy," Owen says with a sly smile. "After he gave his curtain speech, the audience was hoodwinked by his charm. He knew his off-stage charm could be used to advantage on stage."

Owen Phillips again co-stars with Dorothy LaVern in a '50s Barter production.
(Photo courtesy of the Barter Theatre)

"We once toured *The Virginian* with Bob in the featured role. Well, one night he had trouble with his lines and he yelled to the wings, 'Hey, honey, what's my lines here? What's my line here?' Then he got up, walked over, got his line and said, 'Thank you.' The audience loved it and applauded him. He was the only one who could get away with something like that." Owen Phillips pauses, stares for a moment then smiles. "I knew that was no great tragedy in the American theater."

Two actors Phillips felt and feels strongly about are Ernest Borgnine and Ned Beatty—and for similar reasons.

"Honesty was his (Borgnine's) secret," he explains. "The moment he opened his mouth, I could tell he was honest as the day is long. He said, 'I'll do anything you say to become a good actor. I want to learn. You just teach me what to do.' That open face of his has done more for him than anything else. Ned Beatty was another natural, relaxed performer. You never saw it coming with Ned. It just came out the right way."

On a table in Owen's sitting room is a fairly new pictorial biography of Tennessee Williams. The inscription to Owen refers to some fabled dance of long ago. The director chuckles and explains:

"When we were doing *The Milktrain Doesn't Stop Here Anymore*, Bob invited Tennessee Williams and me out to Twin Oaks. Well, we were drinking and Williams and I did a satire on a minuet. Bob loved it. Ever since that time, he says something to me like 'keep dancing.' Williams had seen two Arthur Miller plays I had directed down in Florida, *The View From the Bridge* and *The Crucible*. The next day I got a phone call and the man said, 'This is Tennessee Williams.' I said, 'Oh, sure.' "

Today, Phillips is Barter's beloved ambassador. He can often be seen taking tickets in the foyer of his Barter Theatre, greeting regulars and tourists who make up the summer audiences. Occasionally, he appears in shows. He relishes working the Barter apprentices on children's shows or sharing ideas with young company members.

"We all owe so much to so many people in this business," he points out. "Repay? You can't repay them. You can only try to help someone else."

Owen also takes time to lecture at area colleges about Barter and Bob.

"His death was such a blow to me. It's a void that's never been filled. One vivid memory I have of Bob is him saying, 'What are you worrying about, St. Rita will take care of us.' There were nights Bob and I got down on our knees and asked for St. Rita's help. Sometimes we'd be watching a dress rehearsal and he'd say, 'If we ever needed that little lady, we need her now.' "

Chapter Nine: The Ghosts of Barter

"You know this place is haunted?"

Those are the very first words spoken by Ned Beatty before an actual interview even began. Sitting in the near-deserted theater where he got his start, Beatty asks the question even with the distance of film triumphs and an Academy Award nomination between he and Abingdon.

He could have been talking about the area, the town or the theater. Abingdon holds on devotedly to its myths, history, memories and traditions. It's "spirit," if you will, emanates the past. So, not suprisingly, Abingdon is a town filled with ghosts...whether real or imaginary. Even a brochure put out on Upper East Tennessee and Southwest Virginia makes note of ghostly happenings in Abingdon:

"There are many ghosts in the mountains...or some do say. There are those in Abingdon who lay claim to having heard the ghostly violinist from the Civil War, a Southern girl named 'Martha' blowing the plaintive tunes of the Confederacy to soothe the pains of a 'Yankee Boy' who had won her heart in his last days. War had been raging the countryside, and the day came when the Yankees torched much of the town. The unknown and nameless youth from the North had been secreted into the lovely Preston home, begun in 1830, and delivered into Martha's care. One night as she played for him, Death came. Now in the old Preston home, much heralded as the famous Martha Washington Inn, there are those who swear that on certain midnights up on the third floor of the stately inn, haunting violin strains still sound for the lost and doomed love...."

A fun piece of fluff to attract the tourists? Very possibly, but the effect is made nonetheless. Spirits, ghosts and supernatural happenings often occur where people expect them to: gloomy old houses, for instance, Gothic mansions, countries where superstitions are stronger than technology. In other words, either psychologically or actually, an atmosphere is created in which the supernatural thrives.

And what better place for ghosts than a theater. Now there's atmosphere for you—the very air charged with emotion poured out by decades of actors. Indeed, theaters have always been notorious for ghost sightings and the Barter is no exception. Several actors pooh-pooh any such notion, but there have been more than enough responsible individuals who have had "experiences" in or connected with Barter to merely chalk it all up to imagination. And, invariably since 1971, someone will look you straight in the eye and say, "I've seen Bob Porterfield."

Most do not say this for effect or just to tell a "good story." They want you to know because they think you care. It's easy to be cynical about it until you examine the range of people and sightings. Without giving way to the sensational, coincidence ends when one hears not scattered but consistent reports of ghost sightings at Barter.

In mass market and scientific studies of the supernatural, theaters are mentioned prominently as prime targets for supernatural stomping grounds. Perhaps the most famous of all theatrical ghosts is the "Man in Gray" of London's Theatre Royal, Drury Lane. Generally spotted at the rear of the upper circle, the Drury Lane ghost has been spotted for two centuries and is described without fail as a dignified gentleman in a long gray cloak. Tradition has it that he appears during runs of shows bound for success. The identity of the "Man in Gray" has never been established, although during the 1800s a secret room was discovered in back of the wall near the spot he most often appears. Workmen effecting repairs on the theater found a skeleton with a knife stuck in its ribs.

England, with its grand history of fog-bound streets, royal intrigue and mysterious legends, is rife with haunted theaters. The Haymarket Theatre is supposedly visited by one of its actor-managers; a "woman in white" was often seen at the old Royalty before it was torn down; Sir Charles Wynham, who built the New Theatre in St. Martin's Lane, was spotted backstage after his death; while the spirit of actress Sarah Siddons is said to haunt the Theatre Royal in Bristol.

What was it that James Hilton said about Abingdon? Something about liking it so much because it reminded him of England.

Although not relegated to Porterfield, most of the "psychic" phenomena surrounding Barter is related to Mr. P.

He has been seen in numerous settings and attitudes throughout the theater—the upstairs lobby, seated downstairs, backstage, and even at the Barter Inn. He has been seen in various styles of dress by strangers and people who knew him, but always wearing something he was fond of—a white dinner jacket, a comfortable sweater, a gray suit. The skeptic will say that such "sightings" occur through the power of suggestion and imagination.

You see, there is a stunning portrait of Bob by Dutch painter Jan Clausing that now graces the inside of the theater. The artist used a photograph of him smiling warmly and seated among the familiar red Barter seats. When the lights go down and they play just right with the colors, it actually looks as if the portrait is coming to life. That's a rather compelling piece of suggestion. No wonder some people think for a moment that they may have seen Bob seated among the audience.

But certain incidents can't be explained so nearly. When a Barter apprentice serving as an usher helps someone to their seats and sees a man in a gray suit at their destination, then looks again to find he's vanished, questions begin to form. How could a youngster who never knew Bob Porterfield describe just such a gentleman? The painting, of course. But Bob is wearing a yellow sweater in the painting donned especially for the occasion. How would this apprentice know

Bob was partial to gray?

Does Barter have its own "Ghost in Gray?" Not always. Cleo Holladay remembers seeing something quite different during the run of *Silent Night, Lonely Night* in October of 1974.

"I had a long, long scene where I had to lie in bed on stage," she recalls "The audience couldn't really see my face, but I could look up from my angle and see the kids in the light booth. One night I looked up at them and in the last row was a man in a white dinner jacket (which Bob always wore on opening nights). I'm convinced it was Bob. I know it was. That was the same night the pipes rattled and we took it as a sign that Bob approved of the show."

"The Ghost in Grey appears when a show is bound to be a success."

A gracious and practical woman, Cleo Holladay is not given to theatrical off-stage posturing, nor does she have a history of psychic experience. She tells you that story because she wants you to know about it.

A director is the last person who wants to be known for any kind of irrational behavior. Producers want trustworthy individuals in charge of their productions. But director Jeff Meredith has no qualms about telling you, "I've seen Bob Porterfield."

"I was out in the alley by the stage door with Tony Partington (Rex and Cleo's son) and I went inside to the backstage area. There's that dark little stairway that leads to the scenery storage area and as I went up, I saw a man sitting on one of the steps. Without even thinking, I nodded and said, "Hi, Mr. Porterfield,' As I passed him I realized what I had said and turned around, but nobody was there. I ran out in the alley—shaken and scared—and got Tony. We both came back, creeping around like two little kids. We didn't find anything, but when we reached the top of the stairs we saw a strange light at the ceiling that disappeared. I've never had any kind of supernatural experience before or since, but there's no doubt in my mind that I saw Bob Porterfield."

"Did you happen to notice what he was wearing?"

"He was wearing a gray sweater."

Not yellow. That's not just coincidence.

Some scientists who accept the possibility of ghosts believe they can be explained as visions left behind at highly emotional times. In other words, when our nervous systems are generating a great deal of energy, it is possible that we may actually give off an aura of some kind. It is this aura that some believe became a halo in religious paintings. That energy may in turn leave an image behind, especially in a place that means a great deal to a person.

This is only theory, remember, but it means that some people may leave actual snapshots behind—and some individuals have a greater perception for such images...they see ghosts. It would also explain why theaters—atmospheres super-charged with emotional energy—are so susceptible to sightings. This theory, of course, has not found favor with believers in a "psychic world." They believe that ghosts are the manifestations of a conscious intellect making contact for a specific reason. Of course, if anyone had a consuming devotion to something, it was Bob to his Barter Theatre.

David M. Lohoefer has perhaps the most chilling story to tell. And, oddly enough, it happened during the run of *Silent Night, Lonely Night* (make of this what you will: this play was staged during the month Bob had died three years earlier). Lohoefer was an apprentice at Barter that year, and he and a friend were taking a walk after leaving the Martha Washington Inn. It was about 2:30 in the morning and the two had stopped to sit on the concrete base of a gate than runs in front of the Inn and faces the Barter. Their casual conversation stopped when Lohoefer noticed a man's figure standing in the upstairs gallery. A hand pulled back one of the transparent white curtains and motioned inward, beckoning them towards the theater.

They assumed that someone was playing a joke on them—possibly another apprentice—and crossed the street to the front door. It was locked, and after knocking several times, they went around to try the stage door which was also locked. Back across the street they went and this time the figure was more visible.

"It was a man in a gray suit," Lohoefer said. "We could make him out by the lights thrown from the street lamps. He was still motioning his hand inward when the door of the Barter Theatre opened. It locks from the inside. We could see into the theater and the ghost light, which has always been white, was red. At that moment, before we could decide what to do, a truck pulled in front of the theater to deliver papers. When it pulled away, the door was closed. We went across, but found it locked again. I could see the ghost light was white."

Lohoefer and his friend immediately headed over to the Martha Washington and called Owen Phillips.

"Owen, you'd better get down here," Lohoefer told him. "There's somebody fooling around inside the theater."

" 'Just relax,' he told us. 'Calm down. It was probably just Mr. P. I wouldn't advise going into the theater. Just go home.' "

Mary Dudley doesn't seem surprised by such sightings. During his lifetime, Bob had a few strange experiences himself. There was that prophetic dream at age ten. And Bob was fond of telling about the time he lost certain papers that were very important to Barter's continued state funding. In a dream, Alice Hilton, who died years earlier, took him up to the Barter Inn room where she used to live and pointed at a particular spot. The next day, Bob went up to the room and in that spot he found the missing papers.

"He had a seventh sense," Mary Dudley noted. "He once called home from work and said, 'There's somebody in the basement.' He insisted I go look, and sure enough, there was someone."

It should also be pointed out, however, that ghostly happenings at Barter predate Bob's death. Ned Beatty's own experience, a scare in the dressing room where many actors have gotten the willies, was back in the '60s. Indeed, many are of the opinion that there are actually two ghosts—one benevolent (perhaps that of Bob Porterfield) and the other frightening. And most chilling experiences at Barter happen backstage or in the dressing room area.

Typical of these experiences is the story told by Barter publicity director Lou Flanigan. It was 1967 and Flanigan was working as a stage manager: "I had been here only a week and I was working on the set for *Hamlet*. This was before the apprentices arrived and I was working at night all alone. The theater was almost completely dark, but dark buildings don't bother me. I'm just not succeptible to any type of supernatural stuff.

"I was working stage-right and the only exit was stage-left. All of a sudden, I felt a presence. I felt that I had to get out of there. I just had this horrible feeling that something was really going to get me. I ran across the stage, threw open the door, ran around the scene dock, down the stairs, into the dressing room area and to the stage door that leads to the alley. If I had turned around and seen it, it probably would have been fatal. It was like it was following me. Then I couldn't get the door open. I started kicking it and finally it opened and I ran up the alley to Main Street. One second more and I'm sure it would have grabbed me. When I looked back, I saw that the stage door was wide open. I knew I had to go back and close it, but it was a full 15 minutes before I could work up my nerve to do it.

"I know it didn't come from the house. It came from the stage behind me. It was the single most terrifying thing that has ever happened to me. Fifteen years later it still shakes me. I just won't go back there alone. And it's not only me."

In fact, to his absolute amazement, Flanigan heard Ned Beatty repeat his story almost word-for-word during a 1981 visit to Abingdon. The only difference is that Beatty was chased from the dressing room.

Others will tell you it's not only the theater, but the fourth floor costume attic of the Barter Inn and the Rehearsal Hall are haunted as well.

Other Barter "happenings" happened away from Barter. Both Owen and Frank Lowe remember a particularly frightening experience in Birmingham, Alabama. They were doing Eugene O'Neill's *Ah, Wilderness!*, with Lowe playing the juvenile role loosely patterned on the playwright as a boy. The theater window faced a courtyard and, in the middle of the first act, the actors heard a horrible scream.

"We all heard it," Lowe declared. "All of us in the company. It came from the courtyard. I wasn't a paragon of concentration, but Owen mouthed some words to me and we somehow finished."

That night, they heard on the radio that Eugene O'Neill had died in New York.

As strange as many of these stories are, it should be noted that in the Barter Theatre itself, nothing tragic or malicious has ever been attributed to supernatural occurences. But happenings do persist.

In 1974, Barter housekeeper Ellen Pietsch, a student of Edgar Cayce's works, told a Roanoke newspaper that she found unaccountable spots of light in the balcony. "It's a little like seeing auras," she said.

The Cave House, bought by Alice Hilton and willed to Porterfield, is another supernatural story connected to Barter. Journalist Karen Olsen conducted a

1979 study of the home built on top of a limestone cave—Wolf Cave. Her conclusion after talking to an equal amount of skeptics and believers: "Yes, the house is haunted. And yes, there used to be a secret staircase from the cave to the third floor of the Martha Washington Inn."

As with most supernatural occurrences, some people will always believe the Barter is haunted, while others will never believe it.

Still others, who have heard the stories but never see anything themselves, are like Lou Flanigan. He may not actually see any ghosts, "but I won't be in the theater alone."

Chapter Ten: A Day in October

There had been warnings. A heart attack in the mid-'60s was the most sobering. But Barter without Bob was inconceivable. That vital energy and warm smile—everybody just expected it would go on and on.

Robert Porterfield died suddenly on October 21, 1971 at his beloved Twin Oaks. Owen had done the curtain speech that night.

The cause was a heart attack after a bout with pheumonia. He was 65.

A stunned theater world and government leaders sent words of sympathy to Mary Dudley and young Jay Bird.

Julie Harris wrote: "Bob was so generous to young actors and helped so many on their way. His warmth and laughter and sunny ways and overwhelming belief in live theater made our world a better place."

From New York, Gregory Peck told of his "warm affection and respect for the memory of Bob Porterfield, a dear friend who first encouraged me to go on in the theater. I haven't to this day recovered from the shock of being put on in the Barter in 1940 in the lead of *Button Button* on two days notice and with 110 pages to be learned. It was a shattering experience but I survived as Bob knew I would. In spite of that Porterfield-induced trauma, our friendship has been constant. Bob gave delight to his friends, and careers to so many young people. I'll always think of him as a sunny smiling man with a weather eye out for a kindness to be done. With love to Mary Dudley, Jay Bird and all good friends of Bob's."

From the White House, President Richard Nixon sent this note to Mary Dudley: "Mrs. Nixon joins me in expressing deepest sympathy to you and your family on the death of your distinguished husband. We hope that you will be comforted by the knowledge that his pioneering efforts in the regional theater movement, which earned him such wide respect, have not only added immeasurably to the cultural life of our nation, but also provided inspiration for generations to come. He will be deeply missed, and affectionately and gratefully remembered by all whose lives he touched. May memories of your life together and pride in your husband's accomplishments strengthen you in the years ahead."

Then Virginia Governor Linwood Holton noted that "The Barter Theatre has been an institute in Virginia for thirty-nine years, and Bob Porterfield was the Barter Theatre. He not only enriched the lives of countless Virginians, as well as other Americans, but through the Theatre he established and the plays he produced, he made the Barter into one of America's foremost training grounds for aspiring actors and actresses. By his death, the theater has lost one of its most

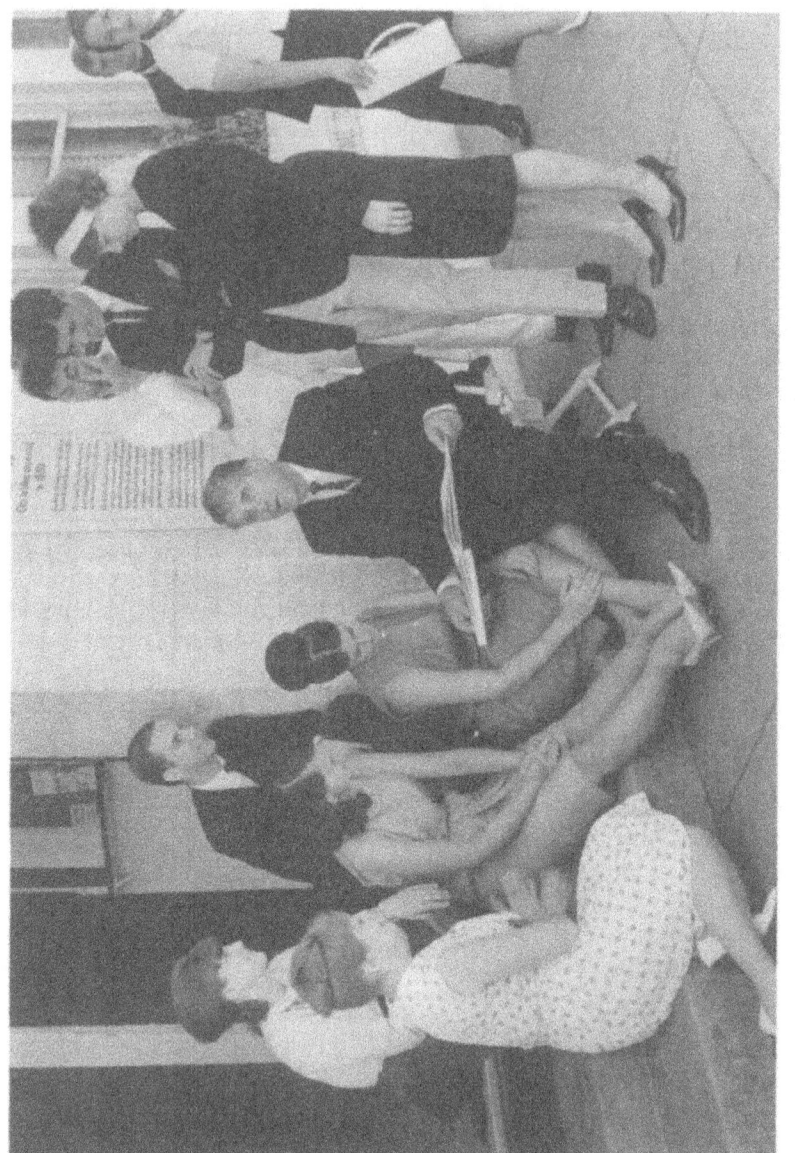

Bob Porterfield surrounded by a '60s company in front of the Barter Theatre.

(Photo courtesy of the Barter Theatre)

dedicated servants."

Ernest Borgnine's message was simple and profound: "Mr. Porterfield did more for me than I did for Mr. Porterfield....No other man contributed as much to the theater as Robert Porterfield."

Robert Pastene, then at the Guthrie Theatre, told of a man who loved so many: "I am blessed to be one of those and hope this message can stand for my presence on this occasion of tribute to an urbane gentleman, a generous teacher, a grave pioneer and an eternal friend."

Larry Gates supplied the following tribute: "And all of us know, Bob would not want us, now, to be sad or dreary. Rather he would tell us his funny stories. He would make us laugh, and we would look forward to more happy achievement, and the many wonderful things he always made happen. We will miss him, but not one of us will ever forget him or his work, the Barter."

From Barter itself came a heartfelt memory. "In my 18 years as executive secretary and business manager to Robert Porterfield and the Barter Theatre," Pearl Hayter wrote, "I am keenly aware of Mr. Porterfield's love for humanity. We are all aware of his love for the theater. He showed his love for humanity in so many ways. He reared a wonderful young man, sent him to college. Walter Mahala is now in England serving his 10th year in the Air Force....Mr. P showed his love by action in so many ways."

A quiet funeral was held at Twin Oaks, with his casket placed beneath the two 600-year-old oaks.

"We had this big Irish Wolfhound," Mary Dudley said. "Bob loved that dog. All during the funeral that dog sat at the head of the casket."

After the funeral, several employees of the Twin Oaks Dairy operation were standing in the yard, waiting to ask Mary Dudley what she intended to do.

"What do you think? We're going to run this farm."

And run it she did; for three-and-a-half years.

"I grieved so terribly for Bob. The farm saved my life. I kept going until I wanted to devote more time to Jay. Now it's leased."

In New York, friends of Bob and Barter gathered at Sardi's for a memorial service. There were those who had helped Bob or had been helped by him—actors, directors, playwrights and producers.

A year after Bob's death, some 400 friends came together in Abingdon for another kind of memorial service. They "bartered" stories and memories of Bob. The next year, Bob's friend Will Geer performed a tribute show at Barter comprised of selections from Mark Twain, Walt Whitman, Robert Frost, Woody Guthrie, John Steinbeck and William Faulkner.

There were other kinds of memorials: the Virginia General Assembly passed a joint resolution expressing "appreciation for a generous and noteworthy life that has contributed so much to the public good," and Virginia's Highway 19 was renamed the Robert Porterfield Memorial Highway.

In the meantime, the Barter Foundation had chosen a successor.

Bob and Jay Bird at Twin Oaks.
(Photo courtesy of Mary Dudley Porterfield)

Chapter Eleven: The Partington Years

For 39 years Bob Porterfield was the Barter Theatre. After his death, a board of directors had to select his successor. Twenty-five people were considered for the position; Rex Partington got the job.

Less the showman and more the efficient artistic director, Partington has committed himself to keeping the Barter growing. Under anyone's direction, the Barter could continue to live off its enormous popularity and considerable reputation. Tourists and residents still would attend the theater simply because it is the Barter.

Yet, Partington quickly established a strong leadership position. The new director let it be known that he would carry on the rich Barter heritage by making sure the company continued to grow artistically.

"I couldn't just be a caretaker," Partington explained. "The fortunate thing is that Robert and I saw eye to eye on about 90 percent of theater matters. A wonderful board of directors has given me a free hand to offer as much as we can as often as we can."

"Bob had spoken to me about Rex," Frank Lowe recalled. "He said, 'You don't know anyone who'd want to take over this thing, honey?' He was looking for someone who could handle all the aspects. I think the right man was chosen. I'm sure Rex has maintained Barter's high standards."

"It's not Bob Porterfield's theater anymore," Bob Gallico noted during his 1980 trip back to Abingdon. "If it ever became the Bob Porterfield Memorial Theater, it would die. He would be the last person who'd want it to become a memorial."

Raised in Queens, New York, Partington studied law at Syracuse University, until the acting bug took hold, and he was graduated with a major in drama. Right after graduation, he was chosen by Shirley Booth for the Barter company in 1950, and he spent two years there before returning to New York.

The young actor struggled in Manhattan, working as a clerk on Wall Street, checking coats, and selling orange juice, among other jobs. After a season at the Arena Theatre in Memphis and some summer stock work, Partington made his Broadway debut in *Lunatics and Lovers*. This was followed by such prestigious engagements as stage manager for *The Matchmaker* and *My Fair Lady*.

Although described by Fritz Weaver as "a powerful, ferocious young actor," he aimed more at off-stage aspects of the theater, serving as production manager for five years at the Guthrie Theatre. Partington eventually formed his own company, Heartland Productions, which toured the Midwest for two years. When the company folded, he took a job as managing director of the Cleveland

A young Rex Partington co-stars with Rosemary Murphy in an early '50s production of **Two On An Island**.
(Photo courtesy of the Barter Theatre)

Playhouse, staying for two-and-a-half years. The year 1971 saw him back in Abingdon as production stage manager. The Board of Directors announced their choice in 1972.

When he took over after Bob's death, Rex was well aware of the size shoes he was stepping into. Bob had already achieved "legend" status and some have only partially joked that it was like taking over for Lincoln.

"There was a great deal of feeling after Bob's death that Barter would close," Partington pointed out. "I suppose the best thing that has happened is that Barter is still going. People come back and their reaction is, 'My heavens, it's still going.' Most everyone was extremely warm and receptive when I started in 1972. Bob was one of the best friends I ever had, but I certainly wasn't going to emulate the man. I had to be my own man or nothing would have worked. Fortunately, I was given artistic carte blanche. I saw my job as trying to continue what he'd been doing—offering a balanced, diversified season—and improving on what had already been established. There was some unspoken resistance from people who wanted Barter to remain exactly the same. I suppose I've lived in Bob's shadow for some time and, to some degree, always will. Had it happened many years earlier when I was sporting a rather fat ego, I don't think I would have been able to do it."

Each January Partington goes to New York and holds open Equity auditions. At the end of the month he holds auditions in Abingdon. A company of about 20 is selected and rehearsals begin if the season is done in repertory. If not, the producing director casts show-by-show, usually retaining several actors for much of the season.

"Historically, the Barter company is a young company," the deep-voiced Partington commented. "But it's nice to have a young company because they have great drive. I think the caliber of actors at Barter has steadily improved and the shows have gotten technically better. The most limiting factor is money."

During his tenure, Partington instituted a repertory program (1979-80), turned the Playhouse into an Equity stage, accepted one of the first Virginia Governor's Awards for the Arts on behalf of Barter, and guided the theater in 1981 to winter quarters on the campus of George Mason University in Fairfax.

"I still feel that Rex was the only person who could have taken over the reigns of Barter," is the admittedly biased opinion of wife Cleo Holladay. "It was fortunate that he had administrative training. And he loves the theater. You see, Bob didn't like to deal with all that administrative crap. Rex likes to be the boss and likes to manage things. When he gets up and says he's heading over to his office for 'a few minutes,' I know he's going to be pouring over books, figures and scripts."

Rex's view of his theater and audience is one of optimism tempered with realism.

"Our audience, while being sophisticated, is a bit on the conservative side," he stated. "That does not preclude me from doing plays of a provocative nature. I owe that to our audience. We must continue to expand. The great works of the

Barter's producing director Rex Partington oversees a photographic session at the theater.
(Photo courtesy of the Barter Theatre)

Director Owen Phillips, playwright Mary Chase and producing director Rex Partington go over the script for **Cocktails With Mimi** *in preparation for its 1973 Barter premiere.*
(Photo courtesy of the Barter Theatre)

past must be done with new plays. Theater must reflect and comment on the times. If I had the money, I would do *Inherit the Wind* right away. We can't be just a summer stock theater or offer dinner theater fare. The works of Arthur Miller and Bertolt Brecht must be done."

Even though acting has been pushed into the background for Barter's producing director, he still tries to appear at least once a year in such roles as John Tarleton in Shaw's *Misalliance* or his riveting portrayal of Dr. Sloper in *The Heiress*.

He also points with pride to Barter's membership in the League of Resident Theaters (LORT), a group of select theaters across the country that includes Lincoln Center, PAF in New York, the Guthrie in Minnesota, Arena Stage in Washington, the Alley in Houston, ACT in San Francisco, and Long Warf in New Haven.

"There have been so many highlights from the last ten years," he said. "Being able to do a 15-week season in Fairfax is one of the most gratifying. With the

Cleo Holladay, center, greets the cast of the 1981 production of **The Royal Family,** *which also featured, left to right, Cynthia Parva, Rebecca Taylor, Russell Gold, Leta Bonynge, Richard Voights and Paul Merrill.*
(Photo courtesy of the Barter Theatre)

Cleo Holladay and Rex Partington as they appeared in the 1981 production of **The Heiress**.
(Photo courtesy of the Barter Theatre)

Ed Bordo, Dorothy Chace, Ann Buckles, David Darlow and Eda Zahl drink up in this scene from the 1973 Barter production of **Cocktails With Mimi.**
(Photo courtesy of the Barter Theatre)

season in Abingdon and touring, it expands our activities as a true State Theatre."

"I really liked the true repertory schedule we did for those two years. It's very stimulating for a company to be playing more than one play at a time. It keeps you on your toes. I'd like to get back to that."

"And I'd still like to do new plays, and aim at more quality actors so we can do Chekhov, or Brecht, or *St. Joan*, or Shakespeare's histories. I'd also like to do more experimental theater in the Playhouse, but we don't have the younger, cosmopolitan audience to support that. We're trying to maintain the tradition and move forward, without losing the sight of how it all started. We still accept barter at the box office, based on current market value of produce."

"Rex has great insight," scenic designer Lynn Pecktal declared after returning to Barter in 1981. "I think Barter has continued to go extremely well because the spirit hasn't changed."

The two men that had the greatest influence on Partington also happen to loom prominently in the history of decentralized theater—Bob Porterfield and Tyrone Guthrie.

"They were friends and inspirations," he said. "Bob was my first influence right out of college and he instilled the ideas of getting the theater to the people. Tony Guthrie stressed quality and excellence. I had the pleasure of doing two Broadway plays with him—one was a success, the other was a flop. He behaved the same in both."

Partington also has some interesting opinions about the future of acting in this country: "I would like to see more respect for the professional theater. From a social standpoint, it should be in the same category as medicine, law and education. The day of the fly-by-night show folk is passing. The actor should be a stoic, responsible individual properly recompensed for his efforts."

No matter where the American theater goes, Rex Partington has proved to Abingdon and the theater world that Barter will continue to meet and set certain standards. Bob Porterfield lives because his theater is alive.

A fine view of Barter interior, including main seating area, balcony and chandeliers.
(Photo courtesy of the Barter Theatre)

Chapter Twelve: The Importance of Being Barter

When the Barter Theatre opened its doors in 1933, it was bad times for the American theater. Broadway was hard hit, so the theater was hard hit. Recent years have seen a period of steady decline for Broadway. Ticket prices have skyrocketed. The number of overall productions is way down. The number of revivals is way up. And profits are way down. But 50 years after the Depression, the situation is not so desperate for the American theater as a whole. Several excellent regional theaters have made sure of that.

Even if one bemoans the lack of quality on Broadway, they can be heartened by the overall picture of health. Indeed, the American theater may be healthier now than ever before. Barter, Bob Porterfield and Rex Partington all have a hand in that development.

For years and years, the rest of the country "fed" off Broadway. After a show left the Great White Way, some areas of the country may have seen it through a touring, regional or community production. Everybody was doing what Broadway had done. Now that's reversed and Broadway finds itself turning to other artistic centers for challenging, innovative shows. Regional theaters are now feeding Broadway. That's been one of the outgrowths and benefits of decentralized theater.

More importantly and specifically, Barter has brought quality theater to an area where it's most needed. Despite its problems, New York, has theater running out of its ear. But Southwest Virginia and Upper East Tennessee—well, enough said. Through 50 years of changes, improvements, setbacks, lean years, innovations, heartbreaks and triumphs, Barter has proclaimed that cultural enrichment is as necessary as the food bartered for tickets in 1933.

In mere statistics, it's easy to say where Barter is today: The Barter players stage about a dozen plays from spring through October in Abingdon, now moving on to 15 weeks in Fairfax, and a major tour. It remains the country's longest-running professional theater and the second-oldest theater structure. Across the street, the Barter Playhouse is the site of mainly musical revues. During the summer, people from Abindgon, neighboring communities and tourists fill the 380-seats of the old Oprey House, with many of the out-of-town theatergoers staying at the Martha Washington Inn.

But in influence and stature, it's not so easy to assess Barter's current status.

Partington carries on Porterfield's tradition of giving away a gift to the person attending for the first time from the farthest distance. On any given night, particularly during the Virginia Highlands Festival, it goes to someone from "outside the continental limits of the United States." It bears out the title of "world famous

Barter Theatre as it appears today.
(Photo courtesy of the Barter Theatre)

Barter Theatre" and is one indication of where Barter is today.

Betsy Graham of Bristol remembers trading 12 ears of corn in the late '30s to see *He Who Gets Slapped*. Now she buys a ticket like everyone else. How has Barter changed? "At the beginning it was a folksy, hometown community theater. Now it is a place to see and be seen. It is a tourist attraction and that's where most of the houses come from."

Good or bad, that's also where Barter is today.

"Barter deserves and needs recognition," declares Cleo Holladay. "Especially locally. There are people in London who know the Barter Theatre and on Main Street there are people who have lived here all their lives and never stepped foot inside the theater."

Barter's influence may be more profound than even Bob would have guessed. In addition to its integral role in the regional theater movement, Barter has also contributed to growth of theater in Southwest Virginia and Upper East Tennessee. When Barter was founded in 1932, there was only one community theater in existence, the Johnson City Community Theatre. Today that area is known as the Tri-Cities, centering around Bristol, Kingsport and Johnson City, and including such towns as Abingdon, Big Stone Gap, Wise, Pennington Gap, Hiltons, Gate City and Glade Spring, Virginia, and Bluff City, Blountville, Piney Flats, Elizabethton, Jonesboro, Erwin, Rogersville, and Greeneville, Tennessee. In 1982, this area was supporting a professional dinner theater, a professional road company, eight community theaters, two annual outdoor dramas, and seven college or university theater programs. Although Barter can hardly be credited exclusively for such growth, its inspiration and influence is undeniable.

As for the individual actor:

"There are very few theaters like this that provide the environment to learn," says Frank Lowe.

"It's an overview of theater training that has lasted from the Depression until now," adds Lynn Pecktal.

"There is a tremendous feeling of ensemble," contributes actress Lily Lodge, who appeared at Barter in 1980. "It's idyllic."

With all the tradition and devotion to progress, these are all places Barter is today.

After 50 years, Barter is still an expression of love—for the theater, a town, a region, state and country. It would be impossible to even begin an evaluation of worth or calculation of the many this one small theater in Southwest Virginia has touched. There are many eloquent ways to summarize these accomplishments, but it would be inappropriate to not let Bob Porterfield have his inevitable curtain line:

"If ya' like us, talk about us. If ya' don't, jes keep ya' mouth shut!"

APPENDIX A

A Code of Ethics for People in the Theatre

Dramatic art is the most human of all the arts. We are servants of humanity—the producer, director, dramatist and actor—pledge unanimity in giving the audience the best theatre possible.

We pledge complete loyalty to the theatre, our great and noble profession.

We pledge ourselves not to let our position or our name be used in any way which will bring discredit to the theatre.

We will not speak derogatorily to the layman about our fellow actors, producers, dramatists. It is bad business to talk bad business in show business.

In theatre, where illusion is the first of all pleasures, we pledge our God-given talent for the reflection of life in all its respects, through comedy and tragedy, magic and glamour, and the world of make-believe.

We pledge ourselves to do everything possible to enhance our art and artistry and the theatre as an institution.

We recognize the producer as the autocratic head.

We pledge our talent to the dramatist in portraying his story of yesterday, today and tomorrow.

We pledge our acquiescence to the interpretation of the director.

We pledge ourselves to respect, cherish, and nourish the artistry of the actor.

It is our duty to appeal to the gregariousness of man, and to him we pledge the propagation of the eternal verities.

In humility we recognize the pleasure of our audience as the final criterion because without an audience we cannot have theatre.

(Note: This code was prepared by Robert Porterfield in 1957 with the help of theater friends in New York. It uses the old style English spelling of "theatre" throughout.)

APPENDIX B

The Aims and Purposes of the Barter Theatre

It is to serve as non-profit educational and cultural expression for the purpose of giving the people of Virginia, and its many guest-tourists, an opportunity to observe some of the works of the world's most distinguished playwrights, performed by competent actors.

It is to bring good entertainment to the people of Virginia.

It makes it possible for the young actors, young writers, and young technicians of the theatre to get practical experience in the Arts of the Theatre, working in cooperation with experienced professional actors, writers and technicians.

To make it possible for tourists traveling through Virginia to see "after-dark" entertainment after they have seen Virginia's day-light scenery—the drives, the gardens, the historical shrines.

The primary purpose is that Virginia have its own standard of appreciation of the theatre, differentiated from the tradition of the theatre.

It is to be a living example of Democracy at work, carrying out the fundamental principles of Virginia's Bill of Rights.

The lobby of the legitimate theatre is the only institution that serves as an example of pure democracy, because the legitimate theatre is the only institution still left where all creeds, classes and political faiths can gather under one roof and have a mingling of social graces, manners, and customs.

We must erect a defense against the evils that would destroy the culture and enlightenment of the world, and this is not to be done by the mechanism of munitions and men and steel alone, but by giving the best of our strength and devotion to the cause of a deeper faith of truth and beauty, and the wisdom of the human soul.

"We hope to avail the State of those talents which nature has sown so liberally among the poor as the rich, but which perish without use, if not sought for and cultivated."

--Thomas Jefferson

(Note: The "Aims and Purposes" was prepared and printed in summer programs of 1941 when it looked as if Barter would become the State Theatre.)

APPENDIX C

The Barter Theatre Award

Winners and audition selections

Year	Winner	Audition selections
1939	Laurette Taylor	Larry Gates, Edith Sommers
1940	Dorothy Stickney	Gregory Peck, Evelyn Wells Fargo
1941	Ethel Barrymore	Robert Pastene, Charlotte Wilson
1942	Mildred Natwick	Paul Wasserman, Margaret Phillips
1943	Tallulah Bankhead	no audition, theater closed for war.
1944		NO AWARD PRESENTED
1945		NO AWARD PRESENTED
1946	Louis Calhern	Martin Waldron, Joan DeWeese
1947	Helen Hayes	Ray Boyle, Marion Wilson
1948	Henry Fonda	James Andrews, Virginia Baker
1949	Tallulah Bankhead	Robert Blackburn, Patricia Larson
1950	Shirley Booth	Jerry Rifkin, Gaby Rodgers
1951	Frederic March	A. Hedison, Rosemary Murphy
1952	Cornelia Otis Skinner	Charles Quinlivan, Sylvia Short
1953	Rosalind Russell	Charles McCawley, Grant Williams, Jane Moncure
1954	David Wayne	Paul Lukather, Phyllis Wynn
1955	Mary Martin	Jerry Hardin, Cleo Holladay
1956	Julie Harris	Arne Sundergaard, Marcie Hubert
1957	Ethel Merman	Mitch Ryan, Vienna Cobb Anderson
1958	Ralph Bellamy	Alex Murray, Elizabeth St. Clair
1959	Robert Whitehead	William Corrie, Virginia James
1960	George Abbott	Donald Linaham, Diane Hill
1961	Hume Cronyn	Gene R. Coleman, Joan Lancaster
1962	Abe Burrows	Gerome Ragni, Tojan Matchins
1963	David Merrick	Michael Bierne, Melinda Dotson
1964	Robert Preston	Robert Jundeland, Daryle Ann Corr
1965	Roger L. Stevens	Russ Murphy
1966		NO AWARD PRESENTED
1967		NO AWARD PRESENTED
1968	Tom Prideaux	NO AUDITION
1969	Pearl Bailey	NO AUDITION

(Note: The Barter Theatre Award was originally intended to honor what was judged the best performance of the theatrical season. Later, Porterfield loosened the eligibility to recognize the contributions of playwrights, producers and directors.)

APPENDIX D

Awards and Honors Presented to Robert Porterfield and the Barter Theatre

February 17, 1939: Life appointment as an Honorary Colonel in the Virginia Militia for contributions to the state's cultural life. Presented by the First Families of Virginia Association.

March 28, 1949: Antoinette Perry (Tony) Award for contributions to the American theater.

June 1, 1948: Honorary Doctor of Literature from Hampden-Sydney College.

June 10, 1957: Named First Citizen of Abingdon by Town Council.

September 24, 1957: Actors' Fund Award of Merit

September 27, 1963: Thomas Jefferson Award for public relations on behalf of Virginia. Presented by the Old Dominion Chapter of the Public Relations Society of America.

March 4, 1967: Suzanne Davis Memorial Award for contributions to the theater in the South. Presented at the Southeastern Theatre Conference.

May 1, 1967: Special Service Award presented by the Virginia State Chamber of Commerce in Arlington.

March 6, 1972: General Assembly of Virginia House Joint Resolution No. 105 "On the death of Robert Huffard Porterfield" as "evidence of the abiding regard which he earned in the hearts of all Virginians."

November 16, 1979: Special Award presented to the Barter Theatre at the First Governor's Awards for the Arts in Virginia. Accepted by producing director Rex Partington in Richmond.

BIBLIOGRAPHY and REFERENCES

Although much of the information in this volume is the result of interviews, several publications were invaluable in researching Barter and the many aspects of theater it encompassed. Perhaps the greatest resource for the Barter student is the scrapbooks stored in the Barter Inn. These volumes are kept year to year, and, as one would expect, some are more complete than others. For the most part, however, the scrapbooks contain most reviews, programs, posters, newspaper articles, magazine features and any other clippings pertinent to that season.

THESES

Keller, Theresa Diane. *A Survey of the Attitudes of the Abingdon Community Towards Barter Theatre of Abindgon, Virginia*. (Greensboro, North Carolina, 1977) A thesis submitted to the faculty of the graduate school at the University of North Carolina in partial fulfillment of the requirements for the degree of Master of Arts.

Williams, Anne St. Clair. *Robert Porterfield's Barter Theatre of Abingdon, Virginia; The State Theatre of Virginia*. (Urbana, Illinois, 1970) Thesis submitted in partial fulfillment of the requirements for the degree of Doctor of Philosophy in Speech in the Graduate College of the University of Illinois.

BOOKS

Archer, Fred. *Exploring the Psychic World*. New York: William Morrow and Co., Inc., 1968.

Atkinson, Brooks. *Broadway*. New York: McMillan Publishing Co., Inc., 1974.

Barbour, Alan G. *Humphrey Bogart*. New York: Pyramid Publications, Harcourt Brace Jovanovich, 1973.

Baumol, William J., and Bowen, William G. *Performing Arts: The Economic Dilemma*. New York: Twentieth Century Fund, 1966.

Blum, Daniel. *A New Pictorial History of the Talkies* (revised and enlarged by John Kobal). New York: G.P. Putnam's Sons, 1973.

Brooks, Tim, and Marsh, Earle. *The Complete Directory to Prime Time Network TV Shows: 1946-Present*. New York: Ballantine Books, 1979.

Farrell, Barry. *Pat and Roald*. New York: Random House, 1969.

Freedland, Michael. *Gregory Peck*. New York: William Morrow and Co., Inc., 1980.

Gard, Robert E.; Blach, Marston; and Temkin, Pauline. *Theatre in America: Appraisal and Challenge*. Madison, Wisconsin: Dembar Educational Research Services, Inc., and New York, Theatre Arts Books, 1968.

Green, Abel, and Laurie, Joe, Jr. *Show Biz: From Vaude to Video*. New York: Henry Holt and Company, 1951.

Houghton, Norris. *Advance from Broadway: 19,000 Miles of American Theatre*. Freeport, New York: Books for Libraries Press, 1971.

Hughes, Glenn. *A History of the American Theatre, 1700-1950*. New York: Samuel French, 1951.

Hyams, Joe. *Bogie: The Biography of Humphrey Bogart*. New York: The New American Library, Inc. 1966.

Langer, Lawrence. *The Magic Curtain*. New York: E.P. Dutton and Company, Inc., 1951.

Langley, Stephen. *Theatre Management in America*. New York: Drama Book Specialists, 1974.

Lewis, Alan. *American Plays and Playwrights of the Contemporary Theatre*. New York: Crown Publishers, Inc., 1965.

Little, Stuart W., and Canton, Arthur. *The Playmakers*. New York: W.W. Norton and Co., Inc., 1970.

Maltin, Leonard (ed.). *TV Movies: 1981-82 Revised Edition*. New York: The New American Library, Inc., 1980.

Marx, Groucho. *Groucho and Me*. New York: Manor Books, 1974.

Novick, Julius. *Beyond Broadway: The Quest for Permanent Theatres*. New York: Hill and Wang, 1968.

O'Connor, Richard. *Heywood Broun*. New York: G.P. Putnam's Sons, 1975.

Skinner, Corneilia Otis. *Life With Lindsay & Crouse*. Boston: Houghton Mifflin Company, 1976.

Teichmann, Howard. *George S. Kaufman: An Intimate Portrait*. New York: Atheneum, 1972.

Thomas, Tony. *Gregory Peck*. New York: Pyramid Publications, Harcourt Brace Jovanovich, 1977.

Williams, Tennessee. *Memoirs*. Garden City, New York: Doubleday and Company, Inc., 1975.

Ziegler, Joseph Wesley. *Regional Theatre: The Revolutionary Stage*. Minneapolis: University of Minnesota Press, 1973.

NEWSPAPERS

Several regional newspapers have covered Barter activities quite extensively throughout the years. Among those most helpful in the preceeding research were the *Bristol Herald-Courier, Bristol Virginia-Tennessean, Bristol News-Bulletin, Kingsport Times-News, Johnson City Press Chronicle, Washington County News, Abingdon Virginian, Sullivan County News, Gate City Herald, Big Stone Gap Post, Elizabethton Star, Stage Post (of Southwest Virginia and Upper East Tennessee), Southwest Virginia Enterprise, Roanoke World News, Roanoke Times, Knoxville Journal, Richmond News Leader* and the *Richmond Times-Dispatch*.

Other newspapers to have run stories on Barter helpful in the preparation of this book include the *Baltimore Sun, Charlotte Observer, New York Times, New York Sun, New York Herald-Tribune, New York Evening Post, Washington Post, Washington Evening Star* (earlier the *Star-News*), *Atlanta Constitution, Los Angeles Times, Variety* and the *London Times*.

MAGAZINES

"Actors and Hams." *Time*, XXXIV, No. 14 (October 2, 1936), p. 38.

"The Actors Are Come Hither." *Time*, LIII, No. 24 (June 13, 1949), pp. 76-77.

Ardinger, John. "Barter Theatre's Exciting Season." *The Commonwealth*, XX, No. 11 (November, 1953), pp. 25-27.

"Baa Baa Mr. Porterfield." *Forum*, June 24, 1936, p. 2.

"Barn to Broadway." *Theatre Arts*, XXXVII, No. 10 (October, 1953).

"Barter." *Cue Magazine*, July 18, 1936, p. 20.

"Barter is Twenty-Five." *Theatre Arts*, XLI (October, 1957), pp. 59-62.

"Barter Theatre Trades Drama for Ham and Eggs." *Life*, VII, No. 5 (July 31, 1939), pp. 54-55.

Breen, Robert, and Porterfield, Robert. "Toward a National Theatre," *Theatre Arts*, XXXIX (October, 1945), pp. 599-601.

Clark, Margy. "Two Years after Porterfield: where does Barter Theatre Stand?" *Weekender (Kingsport Times-News* magazine), July 27, 1974, pp. 2-3.

Dawidziak, Mark. "Barter Theatre: Bob Porterfield's Brainstorm." *Commonwealth Magazine*, Vol. 48, No. 3 (March, 1981) pp. 56-63.

Dawidziak, Mark. "Barter Theatre: The History and the Heritage." *Saturday Magazine (Bristol Herald-Courier)*, June 9, 1979, p. 3.

Dawidziak, Mark. "The Stars at Barter." *Weekender (Kingsport Times-News* magazine), July 24, 1981, p. 2-4.

Dorsey, John. "Barter Theatre: Still Swapping Tickets for Food." *Sunday Magazine* (The *Baltimore Sun*), August 2, 1964, pp. 12-14.

Friddel, Guy, "Old Dominion Foundation Grants Aid Abingdon." *The Commonwealth*, December, 1967, pp. 35-40.

Kent, Arthur T.S. "Bring Your Beans and See the Show." *The Commonwealth*, II, No. 8 (August, 1935), pp. 9-10.

Kiss, Tony. "Inside Barter Theater." *Weekender (Kingsport Times-News* magazine), April 21, 1979, pp. 2-3.

Millstein, Gilbert. "The Importance of Being Marty." *Colliers*, CSSSVI, No. 2 (July 22, 1955), pp. 48-53.

Moustakis, C.C. "Giving the Theatre Back to the People." *Readers Digest*, XXIX, No. 170 (June, 1936), pp. 97-98.

"New Horizons for the Summer Theatre." *New York Times Magazina*, August 2, 1936, pp. 24-26.

Olson, Karen. "Where Mystery Meets History: The Haunting of the Cave House." *The Plow*, August 13, 1979, pp. 24-26.

Plawin, Paul. "Professional Theatre has Thrived for 35 Years in Tiny Abingdon, Virginia." *Southern Living*, April, 1967, pp. 30-31.

Porterfield, Robert. "How Living Theatre Won State Legislators." *Theatre Arts*, XL, No. 10 (October, 1956), pp. 512-513.

Porterfield, Robert. "Trouping Shakespeare." *Theatre Arts*, XXV, No. 4 (April, 1951), pp. 55, 90-92.

Sale, Marian Marsh. "Porterfield: Virginia's Man of the Stage." *The Commonwealth*, June, 1967, pp. 62-65.

"Southern Farmers Swap Country Produce for City Plays." *Newsweek*, June 20, 1936, pp. 24-25.

"Theatre Arts Spotlights: Robert Porterfield." *Theatre Arts*, XXXVI, No. 6 (June, 1952), p. 23.

Vernon, Grenville. "The Play." *The Commonwealth*, January 25, 1935, p. 23.

Williams, Dr. Anne St. Clair. "The Barter Theatre: A History." *Southern Theatre*, XV, No. 3 (March, 1972), pp. 5-19.

Williams, Alton. "State Theatre in Action." *Theatre Arts*, XXXL, No. 7 (July, 1947), p. 62.

UNPUBLISHED SOURCES

Some of the most informative materials in preparing this text are publications from the Barter Theatre, the Abingdon Chamber of Commerce, and the State of Virginia.

Abingdon, Virginia: 200 Years. A pamphlet put out by the Washington County Chamber of Commerce that includes "A History of Abingdon, Virginia" by Walter H. Hendricks.

Historic Abindgon. A pamphlet overview of Abingdon, Damascus and Glade Spring published by the Washington County Chamber of Commerce.

Land of the Mountains: Upper East Tennessee and Southwest Virginia. A full color pamphlet-sized tourism fold-out giving overview of the Tri-Cities area.

Upper East Tennessee & Southwest Virginia: A Quiet Retreat You Can Still Afford. A booklet on the Tri-Cities prepared by Edwards and Associates Advertising.

Virginia Highlands Festival. A pamphlet outlining the festival.

Washington County Virginia: Business Directory and Community Guide. A booklet printed by the Washington County Chamber of Commerce.

Barter Theatre publications:

The Barter Story: 1933 to the Present. A Nov. 1, 1975 four-page history of Barter.

Barter Theatre Buildings. A one-page overview by Lucy H. Bushore.

Barter Theatre, Abingdon, Virginia. A fold-out brochure including a reprint of Joseph R. Judge's *Amerika* story on Barter.

Barter Theatre: 1980 Newsletter. Four-page publication prepared by publicity director Lou Flanigan.

Barter Theatre: Fall, 1981 Newsletter.

Barter Theatre: 1979 Repertory Program. Booklet-form program that includes brief articles on Abingdon and Barter.

Barter Theatre: 1980 Repertory Program.

Barter Theatre: The 1981 Season. Booklet program for ten-play season prepared by Lou Flanigan.

A Brief History of Barter. One page summary.

The Famous Barter Theatre. An over-sized booklet reprinting articles on Barter and serving as the program for *The Virginian*.

Barter Theatre. Over-sized booklet with numerous articles and pictures from Barter's past printed for 1960 season.

Robert Porterfield: A Memorial. Booklet in honor of Barter's founder that includes a text by Jim East, historical photographs, and a list of Barter Award winners.

Robert Porterfield Announces the Opening of the Barter Theatre's 17th Season. A 1949 pamphlet-size brochure.

Robert Porterfield presents the Barter Theatre. A 1960's brochure.

Visit the World Famous Barter Theatre. A 1970s brochure.

Minor's Printing, Boone, NC

ABOUT THE AUTHOR

MARK DAWIDZIAK has been a theater, film, and television critic for more than thirty-five years. He has been the TV critic at the Cleveland *Plain Dealer* since 1999. His many books include the horror novel *Grave Secrets* and such nonfiction works as *The Bedside, Bathtub & Armchair Companion* to *Dracula* and two acclaimed histories of landmark TV series: *The Columbo Phile* and *The Night Stalker Companion*. Five of his books are about Mark Twain.

www.ingramcontent.com/pod-product-compliance
Lightning Source LLC
Chambersburg PA
CBHW031151160426
43193CB00008B/326